LEARNING
TO THINK
THINGS
THROUGH

A GUIDE TO CRITICAL THINKING
ACROSS THE CURRICULUM

Gerald M. Nosich

Prentice
Hall

Upper Saddle River, New Jersey 07458

DEDICATION *To Matt*
and to my I-Group, Mickey, Francis, Mari, Gus

Library of Congress Cataloging-in-Publication Data

Nosich, Gerald M.
    Learning to think things through : a guide to critical thinking across the curriculum /
Gerald M. Nosich.
        p. cm.
    Includes bibliographical references and index.
    ISBN 0-13-030486-7
    1. Critical thinking—Study and teaching. 2. Interdisciplinary approach in education. I.
Title.

LB1590.3 .N67 2001
370.15'2—dc21

                                                                        00-066542

Acquisitions Editor: Sande Johnson
Production Editor: Holcomb Hathaway
Director of Manufacturing and Production: Bruce Johnson
Managing Editor: Mary Carnis
Manufacturing Manager: Ed O'Dougherty
Art Director: Marianne Frasco
Marketing Manager: Christina Quadhamer
Marketing Assistant: Barbara Rosenberg
Editorial Assistant: Cecilia Johnson
Cover Design: Kiwi Design
Composition: Aerocraft Charter Art Service
Printing and Binding: The Banta Company

Prentice-Hall International (UK) Limited, *London*
Prentice-Hall of Australia Pty. Limited, *Sydney*
Prentice-Hall Canada Inc., *Toronto*
Prentice-Hall Hispanoamericana, S.A., *Mexico*
Prentice-Hall of India Private Limited, *New Delhi*
Prentice-Hall of Japan, Inc., *Tokyo*
Pearson Education Singapore Pte. Ltd.
Editora Prentice-Hall do Brasil, Ltda., *Rio de Janeiro*

Prentice
Hall

10   9   8   7   6   5   4   3
ISBN 0-13-030486-7

Contents

CHAPTER 1

What Is Critical Thinking?   1

Standards of Critical Thinking   117

Putting It All Together:
Answering Critical-Thinking Questions   149

To the Instructor

This book is intended as a guidebook for learning to think critically in a discipline, a subject matter, an area, or a field of study. I use these terms more or less interchangeably throughout the book. It applies to disciplines taught at any level of generality, at any educational level. This includes courses in humanities, social and natural sciences, business, arts, nursing, international studies, and so on. It includes multidisciplinary courses, but it is in no way confined to them.

I specifically mean to include courses that emphasize *doing* as well as *understanding*: composition courses stand out in particular. (There are exercises suitable for student writing, and the text promotes full integration of the composition course with other courses students are taking, across the curriculum.) But the book applies to *any* discipline that emphasizes mindful *doing*: physical education, nursing, business, math, veterinary science, agriculture, foreign languages. (In fact, in the purest sense, *all* courses emphasize doing: learning physics is learning to *do* physics. Learning physics is learning how to *actively* think one's way through the physical world.)

Although this book was not written to be the main text in a course specifically in critical thinking, I have used it that way in my own courses, and many teachers of critical thinking have used Richard Paul's model in their courses.

In my critical-thinking courses, I have asked my students to use the model to analyze and evaluate newspaper editorials; to apply it to problems in their personal lives; to analyze their relationships with other people; to analyze, compare, and evaluate news sources and advertising; to evaluate their own study skills; to think through art works and a wide variety of other topics. Several times I have taught my critical-thinking course where the only other texts required were the texts from *other* courses the student was taking. There, the goal was to help the students learn to think through the disciplines or subject matter they were studying in those other courses. What permits this diversity is the great flexibility of Paul's model of critical thinking.

This book is a guide to critical thinking across the curriculum and is intended to be inexpensive, so that it can be used economically as an adjunct text in a course. I have tried to keep it short enough so that students can be required to read it all the way through near the beginning of the semester. That way they can refer back to it again and again, applying specific critical-thinking concepts to different parts of the subject matter as the course moves along, gradually coming to integrate those parts. *Learning to Think Things Through* works best, I believe, when used in a course that has *another* text. In most cases, that will be the main required book for the course, but it needn't be. The "text" can consist of readings brought in by the teacher or by the students. It can be video or audio material of any sort. It can include chapters, specific problems, case studies, primary sources, journal articles, virtually any outside material. Many questions in this book direct students to apply critical-thinking concepts to the texts in the course.

Many teachers in a field or discipline want their students to learn to think critically about the subject matter they are studying, and to learn to think about the world in terms of that subject matter. They want their students not to be passive recipients of information absorbed from the teacher or the text. Rather, teachers want their students to become active learners who pay attention to crucial elements of reasoning, such as assumptions, purposes, implications and consequences, and who do this in a way that meets high intellectual standards. This book is intended to help accomplish those goals.

Using *Learning to Think Things Through* in a Course

This book can be used by teachers in a range of ways. The way of using the text that I favor is as a highly integrated part of the course as a whole. The goal, again, is to keep students actively thinking their way through the course and the subject matter, rather than sinking back into being passive recipients.

As the teacher, I can have them identify key concepts of the discipline for each chapter, unit, lesson, lecture, and presentation. I can have them construct applications of the concepts from their own experience, integrate the concepts, and draw up concept maps. Students can be given frequent practice at formulating key questions, finding relevant information, evaluating its significance, and searching for alternatives. I can have the students analyze readings or important course material right from the beginning of the course.

In addition to giving students ongoing practice at thinking critically within the discipline, activities like these furnish the teacher with valuable insight into where exactly their students *are* in the course. These activities can be done in group work or individually, in class or as homework assignments, in written or oral form, with or without specific feedback from the teacher. Activities like these, and many others, are identified in *Learning to Think Things Through*, and there are exercises on such thinking activities at the end of each chapter.

There are any number of other ways this book can be used in courses. Teachers can have students work through the book on their own. Assigning exercises at the end of each chapter (some of which have suggested answers) can significantly help students in their critical thinking with minimal input from the instructor.

Many teachers find it valuable to devote some class time to helping students learn how to assess their own work and the work of fellow students, giving one another critical feedback on the thinking. The elements (Chapter 3) and standards (Chapter 4) are an ideal vehicle for this. Devoting this class time, even though it might seem at first glance to cut down on the amount of time devoted to teaching the discipline, allows teachers to give frequent short written assignments throughout the semester (shown to be highly effective in helping students retain and internalize the discipline) and to make sure students receive at least some feedback on them. It does this without increasing the amount of valuable time the teacher spends on reading and correcting student assignments. The brunt of learning is placed where it ought to be, as a responsibility of the students themselves. Teachers are freer to become the resource and the facilitator of learning that they really are.

The elements, standards, and subject-matter concepts make this task of self-assessment focused and beneficial both for the student being assessed and the student doing the assessing. Both are engaged in doing critical thinking about the subject matter. This book contains exercises specifically on this, and many more can be readily constructed using the elements and standards.

Consider a simple example. One of the elements is *purpose*, and one of the standards is *clearness*. In my courses, I give frequent written assignments. For each of them, I ask students to write down at the top what, in their best judgment, is the purpose of the assignment. This in and of itself helps students to focus their thinking (and to be aware that the assignments in fact *have* a purpose—that is sometimes a surprise!). Then I ask students, in pairs or in groups of four, to assess how *clearly* each statement of purpose was written. That gives students specific critical thinking feedback on an important standard, and the clarity of their responses almost invariably improves. Similar feedback can be given from student to student about *any* of the elements and any of the standards.

One further note on using *Learning to Think Things Through*: the model presented here is a highly integrated model, and there is great benefit in having students read the entire book near the beginning of the course, rather than piecing it out as the course progresses. The flexibility and comprehensiveness of the model are not as available to students when they learn one part at a time and *then* try to get a sense of the whole. After getting a sense of the whole, students can then work on those aspects that give them difficulty.

The Model

This book is built on Richard Paul's model of critical thinking. I wrote *Learning to Think Things Through* because there is no short, connected presentation of this model suitable for use in a subject-matter course. Essential parts of it are set forth in Paul's *Critical Thinking: What Every Person Needs to Survive in a Rapidly Changing World*[1] and in *Critical Thinking: Basic Theory and Instructional Structures.*[2] The model is the one Paul, Linda Elder, I, and a number of other workshop facilitators at the Center for Critical Thinking have used in workshops and academies over the years.

The model has quantitative empirical backing. Jennifer Reed, in her doctoral dissertation, tested Paul's model in history classes at the community college level. It fared well not just compared to a didactic course in history, but compared to an alternative model of critical thinking where the key concepts were taught implicitly rather than explicitly (with no significant differences in knowledge of history content).[3]

Two parts of this model form the core of this book.

1. **Elements of Reasoning.** These are the central concepts of reasoning itself. Paul often describes them as the "parts" of thinking. When I reason through something, I may be trying to do any number of things: I may be trying to see the *implications* of holding a certain point of view, for example, or I may be trying to come to some *conclusion*, based on certain *assumptions* I start out with. I may be deciding that I need more *information* to decide this *question at issue.* I may simply wonder what my *purpose* is in a certain venture, and what *alternatives* there are. All of these, and many others, are examples of trying to reason through something. The elements of reasoning are an attempt to extract the common concepts from this virtually unlimited set of reasoning activities. Thus, to learn to reason is to come to mastery of concepts like implications, point of view, conclusions, assumptions, information, question at issue, and purpose. Concepts like these are elements of reasoning. Chapter 3 is devoted to the elements.

2. **Standards of Critical Thinking.** It can be seriously misleading to say that critical thinking is learning how to think. Critical thinking is learning how to think *well.* It is thinking that meets high standards of quality. Again, there are many ways I can think through something well. I can figure out that one conclusion is more *accurate* than another. I can see implications more *clearly* than I saw them before. I can focus on the most *important* aspects of a problem. I can realize that I've thought through an issue *sufficiently*, and that now it is time to act. The standards are an attempt to formulate the heart of

what constitutes the quality component in critical thinking. Like the elements, the standards are a set of concepts. I think through an issue *well* when I think it through accurately and clearly, when I focus on what is most important to deciding the issue, when I think it through sufficiently. To learn to reason well is to come to mastery not only of the elements, but also of standards like accuracy, clearness, importance, and sufficiency. Concepts like these are standards of critical thinking. Chapter 4 is devoted to the standards.

The general injunction, then, in Paul's model, is this:

> Take any problem, in any area, and think it out using the elements of reasoning and the standards of reasoning.

Developing a greater ability to think in terms of the elements and standards promotes a flexibility that is ideally useful, and maximally transferable, in teaching for critical thinking in subject-matter courses across the curriculum.

In *Learning to Think Things Through*, both elements and standards are applied to thinking within the discipline. Part of this, in any field, is learning to think the way someone in that discipline thinks. That means being able to think in terms of specific systems that are taught in the discipline (Chapter 5). More than that, it means being able to think in terms of those central concepts and questions that lie at the heart of the discipline. These are described in Chapter 2.

My presentation of Paul's model differs from his in a few important respects. I have added *context* and *alternatives* to his eight elements. I have also omitted part of Paul's model. For example, because of space limitations, I have reluctantly omitted discussion of the extremely valuable intellectual traits, such as intellectual courage and intellectual humility.

Putting It All Together

A general picture is presented in Chapter 5. It is a picture of the core process of critical thinking, of answering critical-thinking questions in the subject matter. It is tagged by the acronym **QEDS.** You begin by looking critically at the question being asked (Q). You think it through using the elements (E) and the central concepts and questions of the discipline (D). You assess and revise your thinking using the standards (S).

This core process, common to all areas of thinking, is what makes critical thinking transferable. By internalizing it in your course, students can learn to think more effectively in other courses, in the interconnections between disciplines, and in their lives as related to the disciplines.

Acknowledgments

It is a pleasure to express my gratitude to Richard Paul. I told him I would "try on" his model for a year (1991–92). At the end of the year I found that it had transformed not just the way I taught critical thinking, but the way I thought about my life as well. My debt to Richard goes well beyond this book. Every time we meet I look forward to the vivid, focused intellectual conversations I have with him and Linda Elder. He has been my close friend for many years.

I am greatly indebted to any number of thinkers I have worked with and been close to: A. J. A. Binker, Mike Donn, Bill Dorman, Linda Elder, Bob Ennis, Edward Johnson, Ralph Johnson, Ann Kerwin, Marlys Witte; to those who also gave me their time and critical-thinking examples during the writing of this manuscript: Anne Buchanan, Francis Coolidge, Ines Eishen, Jerel Fontenot, Jennifer Reed, Ian Wright; to Jean Von Ah, who gave me help and encouragement at the beginning of this project; and to the students in my critical-thinking classes.

I want to thank the reviewers for their encouraging and invaluable commentary: Jean Chambers, SUNY-Oswego; Paul Grawe, Winona State University; Jim Pollard, Spokane Falls Community College; and Carolyn Vitek, St. Mary's University of Minnesota; and my editor at Prentice Hall: Sande Johnson.

Any inaccuracies or questionable assumptions in this book are my own.

For deep personal support, I want to thank not only Richard Paul, but also Ralph Johnson, Matthew Nosich, Andy McCaffrey, and the members of my I-Group, Spirit Group, and NOMC.

To the Student

The aim of this book is to help you improve your critical thinking within the subject matter of the courses you are taking. A secondary goal, a byproduct of the first, is to help you improve your ability to think effectively in your life as a whole. The way you use this book is likely to be different from the way you use most books in courses.

First, this isn't a book you can just read through. You can't get better at critical thinking merely by reading about critical thinking—not even if you're a very good reader. You have to *do it*. You have to take problems or questions the text asks and actually think them out as you work your way through the book. At least some of them. In addition, it helps if you can get feedback on your thinking. You have to do this again and again.

That's because what the book teaches is not a body of information. If the book is successful for you, you will be learning *to do* something. That requires more than just learning information, more than just learning skills. It is not just about *how* to think critically— it is about actually *thinking critically*.

Learning to do something cannot be accomplished just by reading about it. You can't get thinner merely by reading about dieting; your basketball or dancing won't improve merely by hearing about how to dance or shoot free throws. Your writing won't improve merely by *learning* that you have to consider your audience—you actually have to *consider* your audience. To improve the way you do something, it takes both instruction (in this case, reading the book, receiving feedback) *and* practice (doing it).

Second, depending on what your instructor says, you may need to read the book all the way through right near the beginning of the course, including doing the thinking work. That's because the book gives a unified overall model for critical thinking, and you have to see how the parts all fit together. In the model presented in this book, you think in terms of the subject you are studying (Chapter 2), the elements of reasoning (Chapter 3), the standards of reasoning (Chapter 4), and putting it all together (Chapter 5). You need to have a grasp of the whole model to think your way through questions in the discipline. In the end, the book promotes a different way of approaching the world—by thinking your way through it.

In some fields you proceed step-by-step, learning a skill well, and only then going on to the next skill (and hoping you don't forget the first one on the way). Critical thinking is different. A major goal of critical thinking is always to keep the whole in mind as you are working through the parts.

So, with this book, it is better to work all the way through to the end and get the big picture even if there are some glaring gaps in your understanding. (If you ponder it for a while, you'll realize that's the way you learned most complex skilled activities: you don't learn batting well and only then begin to learn catching; you don't learn how to shop for groceries by first getting good at writing down what you need, and only then going on to the skills of selecting a store, comparing prices, etc. Instead, you engage in the whole process from the beginning, gradually filling in gaps and improving.)

Third, *Learning to Think Things Through* is not a book that you can work through once and then be done with. Instead, you'll have to refer back to it whenever problems arise for you. After working all the way through it the first time, there *will* be glaring gaps in your understanding of various aspects of critical thinking. When you have trouble with assumptions, for example, you need to reread the section on assumptions in Chapter 3. But also look in the index under "assumptions" for other passages that may help. Do some of the exercises on assumptions, especially those that are starred (*) and have suggested answers in the back of the book. At the end of the course, some parts may still be unclear and confusing. Even if that's so, you can still use the model as a whole. It will still be practical: in the course you are taking, in other courses, and in decisions you have to make in your own life.

Fourth, this is a guide to thinking critically within the discipline you are studying: composition, geology, educational psychology, or business—any field or subject matter. Only a fraction, if any, of the examples in the text and exercises, however, will be from the discipline you are actually studying. It is vitally important that you work your way through them. They have been selected so as to convey critical thinking concepts across the curriculum, to all disciplines.

No technical knowledge is presumed in this book. Except for the discipline you are currently studying, you are not expected to know the specific field being discussed.

Critical thinking *transfers*. If you consciously learn critical-thinking techniques in one field, you may have those techniques available for another field. By the end you may find that your learning in your other courses becomes faster, more in your control, more lasting, and more beneficial for your life outside school.

Finally, in the end you will have to be the judge of whether using the model here improves your thinking. Certainly it won't be all or nothing. Critical thinking is a matter of degree. At the end of the course you should find yourself more often checking for accuracy, identifying assumptions, drawing relevant conclusions, thinking questions out in terms of the fundamental and powerful concepts of the discipline you are studying.

One way to think about the process is to imagine yourself in the hands of a good coach, a critical-thinking coach. This book is the manual the coach is asking you to follow, and the coach will give you feedback along the way.

Who is the coach? Well, in a way, it is your instructor. On a much deeper level, though, it is the healthy, thinking organism within you. In the end, you are going to accept processes and thinking guidelines only if they work for you. You will have to see them pay off—in your studies, in your grasp of the subject matter, in your understanding of your relations with other people—before you incorporate them into your life. But you first have to give them a chance to see if they *do* pay off.

What Is Critical Thinking?

Often, a good way to begin the process of thinking critically about a subject is to do some conscious thinking about it *before* you do any reading or hear any presentations in the subject. Thus, if you are going to study biology or sociology or writing, a good way to begin is with pre-thinking: Write down some of the main ideas you already have about biology or sociology or writing *before* you do any reading or listen to lectures. This allows you to be an active listener rather than a passive recipient of information. It helps you to become aware of your assumptions about the subject so that you can assess them more accurately in light of what you will later read and hear.

Begin by examining your own concept of critical thinking. Before you begin reading this text, respond to the following in a paragraph or two:

1. What is your concept of *critical thinking?*

You can respond to question (1) by giving a definition or a description. An alternative way to address it, though, is to use *examples.*

2. Describe a situation in which you thought through something critically.

3. Describe a situation in which you did not think through something critically.

Some Definitions of Critical Thinking

Here are three definitions of critical thinking by leading researchers. First, Robert Ennis's classic definition:[1]

> Critical thinking is reasonable, reflective thinking that is focused on deciding what to believe or do.

Next, Matthew Lipman's definition:[2]

> Critical thinking is skillful, responsible thinking that is conducive to good judgment because it is sensitive to context, relies on criteria, and is self-correcting.

Finally, in informal presentations, Richard Paul uses this definition:[3]

> Critical thinking is thinking about your thinking, while you're thinking, in order to make your thinking better.

Each of these is an excellent definition of critical thinking. It pays to read them several times and to stop and reflect on every aspect of each definition. Why did the expert include this word rather than another? Just what is it that the experts are trying to capture with the words they have chosen? What overlap is there in the definitions, and what main differences of emphasis are there?

It may seem hard to believe, but each of these definitions, brief as they are, is the product of a long period of intense pondering about how best to describe critical thinking. Each definition is an *attempt* to convey in words the essence of an activity, a "thing"—critical thinking. Before trying to define it, each expert had an intuitive grasp of what critical thinking is based on years of working with it. This was what they tried to capture in the words they chose.

So in reading the experts' definitions and in the discussion ahead, one very important goal to keep in mind is for you to develop a solid intuitive grasp of just what critical thinking *is* and what it *is not*.

> Revisit your concept of critical thinking over the course of the semester, and then change it (maybe scrapping it entirely and starting over) so that it accords with your deepening grasp of what critical thinking is.

Some Prominent Features of Critical Thinking

Critical Thinking Is Reflective

Critical thinking is different from just thinking. It is metacognitive—it involves thinking about your thinking. If I enter a social studies course where one of the topics to be studied is *conformity*, it is likely that I already have views about conformity: what it is, how prevalent it is, what influences people to conform or not conform. I have these views even if I haven't formulated them explicitly for myself. Each view is an example of thinking, but not necessarily an example of *critical* thinking. Critical thinking starts once I reflect on my thinking: Why do I have these views about conformity? Since my views are really *conclusions* I have drawn, what *evidence* are they based on? How do other people look at conformity differently? What are *their* views based on? How can I tell which are more accurate, their views or mine?

Critical Thinking Involves Standards

Critical thinking involves having my thinking measure up to criteria. I can think about something accurately or inaccurately. I can use evidence that is relevant to an issue or irrelevant, or somewhere in between. When I reason out and try to understand the main ideas in a course I'm taking, I can do so on a superficial level or I can try to understand them deeply, trying to get at the heart of the matter.

Accuracy, relevance, and depth are examples of *standards* or *criteria*. The words "critical" and "criteria" come from the same root, meaning "judgment." For my thinking to be *critical* thinking, I have to make judgments that meet criteria of reasonableness.

Critical Thinking Is Authentic

Critical thinking, at its heart, is thinking about real problems. Although I can reason out puzzles and brain-teasers, the focus of critical thinking comes out far more when I address real problems and questions rather than artificial ones. Critical thinking is far more about what I actually believe or do. It is about good judgment. Puzzles and narrow problems may help occasionally when special skills are to be honed, but even those help only if I consciously transfer the skills to real-life settings. Honing my skills at guessing the endings of murder mysteries is not likely to be good preparation for becoming a criminal investigator. In murder mysteries, *all* the clues are provided, the murderer is one of the characters, and someone (the author) already knows the murderer's identity. None of that is so in a criminal investigation.

Real problems are often messy. They have loose ends. They are usually unclear: clarifying and refining them are part of thinking through them. They often have no single right answer. But there *are* wrong answers, even disastrous answers: there may not be any single right person to take as your partner in life—but there are certainly people it would be disastrous to choose.

Critical Thinking Involves Being Reasonable

There are no surefire rules of reasoning. That is, there are no rules so foolproof that they guarantee your reasoning will be successful. There are guidelines; there are even "rules" sometimes, but these always need to be followed *thoughtfully*, not by rote. They need to be applied with sensitivity to context, goals, practical limitations—a whole host of realities. For thinking to be critical thinking, it must be reasonable thinking.

Compare critical thinking to driving a car. There are rules for good driving (e.g., merge when entering an interstate), but merely following the rules won't make you a good driver. To be a good driver you have to follow the rules *mindfully*. What does that mean? It means, for example, following the rules while being aware that the *purpose* of merging is to allow traffic to flow more smoothly and reduce collisions between fast- and slow-moving cars, that weather and traffic conditions affect how you should merge, and so on. Notice that this is an *open-ended* list of what a mindful driver is aware of while merging.

Here's an example of an authentic problem. Nurse Garcia is speaking: "I am a nurse administrator, and the health-care people in my charge are taking too many days off. This is costing the hospital a lot of money for replacements, it's making everyone's job more difficult, and besides, they are supposed to be *professionals.*" (At this point, you can hear in her voice that she is personally offended by their conduct.) "I tried talking to two of them, but they got defensive right away, and I'm afraid I didn't handle it very well. Nurse Williams, over in pediatrics, said that *she* thought they were angry at hospital management for reducing sick days last year. But that's not *my* fault. And no matter what I do, they can just claim that they *were* sick. What should I do?"

We often long for surefire step-by-step procedures, and the more personally important or threatening a situation is, the more we want foolproof rules. But there *are no* rules that guarantee our thinking will be correct—and that is especially true in very important or threatening situations. There are no rules to tell us if our reasoning is correct, precisely because we must use our reasoning to evaluate rules, rather than vice versa. The only way we can decide whether to follow certain rules is if we use our best reasoning to determine that those rules are *reasonable*, that they lead to reasonable results when followed. Critical thinking is "self-correcting" at least partly because it is the court of last resort. There is no level of greater certainty beneath it that we can use to evaluate our reasoning.

Three Parts of Critical Thinking

Full-fledged critical thinking involves three parts.

First, **critical thinking involves asking questions.** It involves asking questions that need to be asked, asking good questions, questions that go to the heart of the matter. Critical thinking involves *noticing* that there are questions that need to be addressed.

Second, **critical thinking involves trying to answer those questions by reasoning them out.** Reasoning out answers to questions is different from other ways of answering questions. It is different from giving an answer we have always taken for granted but never thought about. It is different from answering impressionistically ("That reminds me of . . ."), or answering simply according to the way we were raised, or answering in accordance with our personalities. It is also different from answering by saying the first thing that comes into our minds, and then using all our power of reasoning to *defend* that answer.

Third, **critical thinking involves believing the results of our reasoning.** Critical thinking is different from just engaging in a mental exercise. When we think through an issue critically, we internalize the results. We don't give merely *verbal* agreement: we actually believe the results because we have done our best to reason the issue out and we know that reasoning things out is the best way to get reliable answers. Furthermore, when we think critically through a decision about what to *do* in a situation, then what follows the reasoning is not just belief, but *action*: Unless something unforeseen occurs, we end up taking the action we concluded was most reasonable.

Asking the Questions

Critical thinking begins with asking questions. If a teacher assigns a homework problem to solve, a good question to ask is "How can I best solve this problem?" Often, though, as students, we don't ask this question at all. Instead, we just jump in and try to solve the problem by any method that springs to mind. Thinking critically about solving a problem, on the other hand, begins with asking questions about the problem and about ways to address it.

There are any number of other good questions to ask:

How do *you* usually begin to solve problems assigned by teachers: reflectively or just by jumping in? Does it vary from one subject to another? How successful is the method you use? If you are often able to solve the problems just by jumping in, without thinking about *how* to solve them, what does that tell you about the problems assigned?

- What are some *alternative* ways of solving the problem assigned?
- What is a good way to begin?
- Do I have all the information I need to start solving the problem?
- What's the purpose behind the problem?
- How does it fit into a real context?
- Can the problem *be* solved?
- Does the problem even make sense?

All of these questions are relevant when a problem is *assigned*. But when teachers assign problems, they have already done a fundamental part of the questioning. Posing a problem *is* asking a question. So, a major part of learning how to think critically is for you to learn to ask the questions—to pose the problems—yourself.

A major part of critical thinking is *noticing* that there are questions that need to be addressed; *recognizing* that there are problems. Often, this is the hardest part of critical thinking. When I personally fail to think critically, this is the way I most often fail: I don't realize that there are questions I should be asking.

This is true not just in school, but in daily life as well. People often do not ask themselves, "How can I best get along with my parents (my partner, my coworkers, my friends) in this situation?" Instead, they continue relating to them in habitual and unexamined ways. If your goal is to improve some aspect of your daily life, begin by asking yourself some questions: What are some concrete things I can do to improve my job performance? to make better grades? to meet new people? to read more effectively? to make the subject matter of this course meaningful in my life?

To be effective, you need to really *ask* these questions. It is not enough just to say the words of the question. In fact, when you look at the questions just posed, they can seem empty. But that's not because they *are* empty questions. Whether a question is empty or not depends a great deal on the spirit in which you ask it. If you ask it in an empty way, just going through the motions, then it's not a genuine question at all, not for you, and it will not be the beginning of thinking critically through that question.

Many people tend to believe that critical thinking is the same as problem solving. The two are closely related, but they are not the same. In problem solving, someone has already identified a problem and *given* it to you to solve. But identifying the problem in the first place is an essential part of critical thinking.

Identify some situations in your life that are problematic, ones that are not going as well as you think they should. Be specific in how you describe them. Don't just say "How can I get along with my friends?" Focus it: "How can I best deal with Arthur when I feel him pressuring me to do X and I really don't think I should be doing X?"

What are some questions you should be asking about those situations but have not yet asked?

Here are some questions that teachers list as ones that students do not ask, but should be asking, in their courses:

- How does what I learn in this course relate to my own experience?
- How can I use what I learn here in my own life?
- Can I think up my own examples?
- How does this subject matter relate to other courses I am taking?
- What is the evidence behind this?
- How do the topics in this course fit together?
- What is the purpose of the course?
- Why?

Finally, people often ask what makes something a good question. Though many approaches to this emerge during the course of this book, in the end a good question is one you really want to know the answer to. (How to approach and answer critical thinking questions is addressed in Chapter 5.)

Reasoning It Out

Though asking questions is necessary to begin critical thinking, merely asking the questions is not enough; the questions need to be answered (or at least addressed). Often we raise questions only to worry about them, or to torment ourselves, or even to put off action, instead of trying to answer them by thinking them through.

For example, a significant number of students have difficulty in math-related fields. They sometimes ask the question, "Why am I so *bad* at math?" They then use this question to make negative judgments about themselves ("I'm just hopeless at math, and I always will be") or about the field ("I don't need to know math to be a good nurse"), or they answer it with unhelpful generalities ("I'm no good at it because of the way I was taught"). Reasoning

Reflect on your educational experience a little. Which of the questions listed by teachers are ones you tend to ask yourself in courses you are taking? Which of them do you never (or almost never) ask?

Try keeping a journal of questions that arise during a course you are taking now. Questions may be about the subject matter itself, about how it affects you (or *doesn't* affect you), about how you can use it, about implications of the course, about the way it is taught, about the assignments given, about assignments *not* given.

it out, however, requires approaching the question in a different way and with a different spirit. It is the spirit of genuinely wanting to figure out a clear, accurate answer to a question that is important to you. Reasoning it out might begin by rethinking the question and then reformulating it in a more neutral and productive way: "What are the main causes of my problems with math, and what are some good ways to begin dealing with them?" You might then read a little about what causes problems in learning math and apply it to your own case. You could talk to counselors about alternative approaches that have helped other students, take seriously what the counselors say, and note any resistance you have to following new approaches. Reasoning it out may not "solve" the problem, but it does provide a significantly better way of addressing the problem than not reasoning it out at all.

There are many ways to try to answer questions other than by reasoning. You can:

- ask someone (and simply accept their answers uncritically)
- answer according to the way you have been raised (and accept that without examining whether it was a healthy way to be raised)
- answer without looking for information even if it's readily available
- answer in accordance with your personality (without examining the extent to which your "personality" helps or hinders you in this kind of situation)
- answer with what first comes into your head

It is easy to misunderstand questions about reasoning. Thus, you might interpret the second item listed as implying that critical thinking is *opposed* to the way you were raised, but that is not what it means. What critical thinking *is* opposed to is acting in the way you were raised, without examining it. For example, someone raised in a family where violence and abuse were taught should not simply follow those values.

The two greatest difficulties in reasoning are not what you might expect. It isn't that people aren't good at reasoning, or that they make mistakes. Everyone is good at it in some areas and not so good in others; everyone makes mistakes; everyone can improve their abilities. But these are not the most crucial difficulties. They go deeper. The first is that, when presented with a problem, people often don't think to reason in the first place. It's just not the usual human reaction to a problem. This is partly because societies do not encourage reasoning as an approach to important questions. The second difficulty is that people often do not know the difference between reasoning

REASONING VERSUS NONREASONING

What are some important differences between a debate and a reasoned debate? between writing a reaction paper and a reasoned reaction paper? between evaluating an essay and giving a reasoned evaluation of an essay?

through something and other ways of responding. As a result, people respond with what *seems* to be reasoning, but isn't.

For example, a discussion is not automatically an example of critical thinking. Often in discussions, each participant says what he or she believes, and that's the end of the matter. In a *reasoned* discussion, on the other hand, listening is as important as speaking. Participants try to understand the reasons behind other people's beliefs, and they try to identify both the strong and weak points of the views expressed. The whole spirit is different.

When I refer to "reasoning things out," I mean reasoning them out *well.* What *does* it mean, then, to reason through something well?

Reasoning itself is drawing conclusions on the basis of reasons. *Good reasoning,* therefore, is drawing conclusions on the basis of reasons and giving due weight to all relevant factors. Relevant factors include the *implications* of drawing those conclusions, the *assumptions* on which the reasoning is based, the *accuracy* of the reasons used, the *alternatives* available, and a number of other elements (Chapter 3) and standards (Chapter 4).

Though it's not difficult to define good reasoning in an open-ended way, the challenge is to spell it out in a way that is *usable by you,* one that lays a foundation so that your ability to reason well can improve and deepen during the rest of your life. A good deal of the rest of this book is devoted to that.

Describe some situations that occur in your life where you usually respond without reasoning at all (e.g., when someone pushes your buttons). Then describe some situations where you tend to reason through your response.

Are there some areas where you are confident that you can tell the difference between good reasoning and poor reasoning? How do you tell the difference?

Believing the Results

Critical thinking, in the fullest sense, results in belief. It even results in action.

Here is an example. A teacher lowers my course grade because I missed too many classes, and I feel unfairly treated. So I raise the question: "*Was* my teacher being fair in giving me this grade?" Next, I reason my way to an answer: I collect information (maybe I ask the teacher about it; I check what the syllabus said about missed classes; maybe I check to see if other students were treated the same way); I consider the teacher's point of view on the issue and her purpose in lowering my grade because of absences. After reasoning it through—reasoning it through *well*, I believe—I come to the conclusion that my teacher was fair in what she did. The next step seems so obvious as not to need stating: I *believe* the results of my reasoning; I believe that my teacher's actions *were* in fact fair.

However, taking this last step isn't always easy. Even after reasoning it out, I may still have feelings of being unfairly treated, and I may still suspect that I *was* treated unfairly.

What is going on in this example is an indication that I have not thought through the issue critically, at least not in a complete enough way. Maybe there are other questions I should be raising ("Could my feelings of being treated unfairly arise from *other* circumstances in my life?" "What concept of *fairness* am I using in my thinking?"). Maybe there are other paths of reasoning I should follow (there are alternative explanations to consider: maybe I am making some unstated assumptions that are influencing my feelings). Or else, maybe I should just believe the results: the teacher *was* being fair and my original estimate of unfairness was really off the mark (and I need to remember that feelings of being unfairly treated, even if they are unjustified, often take time to go away).

Believing the results is a rough test or measure of the completeness of your critical thinking. If you have reasoned something out and come to a conclusion but find you still don't really believe it, that indicates the reasoning is probably not complete. Important factors probably are missing—factors that lead you to resist internalizing the results.

It is more controversial to link critical thinking to *action*. Suppose, for example, I continue to smoke or to eat too many saturated fats despite the fact that I've done a lot of reasoning about the importance of giving them up. Is that a flaw in my critical thinking? If I can state all the compelling reasons but still do not act on my reasoning, is my critical thinking still excellent? Experts in critical thinking disagree on the answer.

The suggestion here is that there is some flaw in the critical thinking. The flaw can lie in how I think about my own body, or about my life, or about the relation between abstract statistics and my chances of survival. I might have an overriding background belief that those statistics don't apply to *me*, or that even though it's important for me to give up smoking, it's not important that I do it *now*. Sometimes you can even get the impression that certain people don't believe that they will ever die. There is a subtle relation between denial and lack of critical thinking, one that has not yet been fully explored.

It is difficult to identify examples of not believing the results of our own reasoning. That's because, paradoxical as it may sound, it's hard to become aware of what we actually believe and don't believe. There are four indicators of when we are not believing the results of our reasoning (but only the last one is even moderately easy to spot in ourselves):

1. I reason something out, but strong emotions arise within me against the result.
2. I find myself believing contradictory things.
3. I believe something very strongly, but I find I am unable to come up with any good reasons for the belief. In fact, I don't think I even *need* reasons. Thinking the opposite seems ridiculous.
4. I reason something out, but my actions do not follow my reasoning.

The following are examples of the first three indicators (but they may not be convincing to you, especially if you share the beliefs in question):

1. ▪ Michael reasons out the issue of capital punishment as a deterrent. He gathers information and concludes that it does not significantly deter murder or other violent crimes. But after his investigation, he feels angry about this, maybe intensely angry. He says, "Maybe that's true, but I'm still in favor of capital punishment because you have to do *something* to stop criminals."

   ▪ Maria, taking a course in gender studies, reasons her way through the argument that there is no non-sexist reason why a woman should adopt her husband's name at marriage. Like Michael, Maria discovers that the more she follows the argument, the angrier she gets.

2. ▪ Pete believes that all cultures and all cultural practices are equally valid. He believes that people do not have a right to say that a particular culture's practices are wrong. But he also believes that it's part of our Western culture to impose our ideas on others, and that it's wrong for us to do that.

   ▪ Most of us believe that everyone should be treated equally, but that does not prevent us from thinking that we deserve special breaks.

An appropriate exercise would be to ask you to identify situations where you do not believe the results of your reasoning, where each of the four cases applies to you. But that is extremely difficult. Can you identify any examples where indicators (1), (2), and (3) apply to you? If you can find even one, that's a major insight into yourself. (It sometimes helps to begin with other people, and then apply the results to yourself.)

With indicator (4), on the other hand, it should be easy to identify some examples of actions you continue to engage in even though your best reasoned thinking tells you that you should not.

3. ■ Some people think that eating dogs, cats, or seagulls is revolting, but that eating cows or chickens is quite reasonable. They believe this despite the fact that all their reasoning shows the cases are identical. They find themselves trying to make up reasons that they know don't work (such as, "Dogs and cats are pets! That's why it is wrong to eat them").

■ In critical thinking presentations, Vincent Ruggiero asks, "Why not turn cemeteries into parks where children can play?" (Can you give a good *reason* against it?) "We're running out of room: why not bury people in the median strips of highways?"

When you've thought through something critically and come to the conclusion that seems most reasonable to *you*, it should follow that you believe it, and that you will end up acting in accordance with that belief.

AN EXAMPLE OF CRITICAL THINKING IN ACTION

Susan's husband was diagnosed with a serious form of cancer, and the doctor who made the diagnosis recommended a method of treatment. They went for a second opinion, and the second doctor diagnosed the same form of cancer but recommended a different method of treatment.

(continued)

When Susan got home, she decided to research the form of cancer her husband had. She had no previous medical training, but she went to the Internet and then to a medical library and began reading medical textbooks. She found that she couldn't understand them well unless she used a medical dictionary while reading. She even found that some of the medical dictionaries were too hard to understand. So she first had to select one that would be most useful for her. She returned to the text-books, and from there she went on to medical journals.

Picture what she is doing on the net and in the library. This is critical thinking in action. She is actively *asking questions* about how to proceed: "Where can I find the information I need? What tools do I need?" And about the journals and the other sources: "How do I understand what I am reading? What exactly are they saying? What alternatives are there?" She is engaged in *reasoning out* answers: she is interpreting what she reads, applying it to her husband's case, and generating more questions to be answered. She is *acting on her reasoning:* she is actively doing the research, in the middle of great anxiety; she is balancing uncertain answers in her head, and accepting the fact that the answers will not be black and white.

Susan spent five full nine-hour days researching. Then she and her husband went back to the doctors, and now she found she could ask very different questions from the kind they asked the first time. Not all the doctors' attitudes toward this were positive. Some resented her question-ing, but she found many who were very helpful. She could ask questions such as, "In a study in the *New England Journal of Medicine* this form of treatment was not found to be so effective against fast-growing cancers of the sort my husband has. Why would you expect it to be effective in my husband's case?"

Again she is asking questions. Again she is not simply receiving answers passively. Rather she is actively engaged in reasoning through them: interpreting the doctors' responses, applying them to her husband's case, anticipating problems that might arise, and generating more ques-tions. Then she and her husband went home and acted on the reasoning. They discussed it at length and decided on a method of treatment.

That's the end of the example. The treatment was successful—or as successful as such treatment is—but that is not really part of the story. Even if the treatment had been <u>un</u>successful, it still would be an excellent example of critical thinking in action. Apart from the critical thinking Susan engaged in on the Internet, inside the library, and with the doctors, she asked a much more fundamental question: "What can I do, in the limited time available, to help make the best decision possible?" She reasoned her way to an answer: "Find out as much as I can about all relevant aspects of the decision." This is not the only possible answer, but it is an eminently reasonable one. Then she did it.

In some respects Susan's course of action seems obvious, at least by hindsight. If I or someone I love contracts a life-threatening disease, obviously I should try to find out as much as possible about it. But in another sense, it is not obvious at all. It is very unusual as a response. Very few people in the same situation take Susan's course of action. Most of us respond by simply choosing a doctor. When we choose a doctor, we tend to do it impressionistically rather than critically. We rate doctors on whether they seem to be reassuring or knowledgeable, without having any real evidence for these judgments, or we let the hospital or our HMO do the choosing for us.

What Critical Thinking Is *Not*

There are a number of widespread misconceptions about critical thinking. These can throw off your understanding of critical thinking and influence the way you develop in your thinking skills.

Critical Thinking and Negativity

CRITICAL THINKING IS NOT NEGATIVE. The word *critical* often has negative overtones. A "critical person" is one who does a lot of faultfinding. To "criticize" someone usually means to say something negative. A "critic" is often thought of as someone who is against something.

But the word *critical* in "critical thinking" has no negative connotations at all. It is related to the word *criteria*: it means thinking that meets high criteria of reasonability. To learn to think critically is to learn to think things through, and to think them through *well*: accurately, cogently, clearly, reasonably. Some people have proposed the term *effective thinking* as a synonym for "critical thinking," and using that term helps some people in removing the negative overtones.

Critical thinking does involve making judgments. Unfortunately, the term *judgment* has also acquired negative connotations in certain contexts. To be judgmental is certainly not to be a critical thinker, and the judgments a critical thinker makes are far removed from being judgmental.

We cannot exist without making judgments. We make judgments all the time, whether we know it or not. People sometimes say, "I just want to accept people the way they are—myself included—without making judgments about them." There can be a lot of wisdom in that approach. It can mean, for example, "I am going to accept people as having the feelings they have, and the reactions they have, without condemning them for it." That is, refraining from making judgments often means refraining from making harsh value judgments. But it can't be generalized to mean "not making judgments at all." To accept people's feelings and reactions as they are involves making a judgment—the judgment that those indeed *are* their feelings and reactions. Critical thinking comes in directly, because accepting people as they are presupposes making accurate, clear, relevant judgments about what their feelings and reactions are. That *is* accepting people as they are, rather than imposing preconceptions on them.

> Using the word *critical* in the sense of *critical thinking,* what would you say are the main earmarks of **critical reading?** What is the difference between reading your text and reading it *critically?*
>
> How about **critical listening?** What is the difference between listening to a lecture in a course and listening to it *critically?*

THE IMPORTANCE OF NEGATIVE FEEDBACK. Another aspect of negativity must be considered. Sometimes our sensitivity to negative feedback gets in the way of our critical thinking. Suppose someone makes a judgment about your work—that it is inaccurate or unclear, or not relevant to the question asked. Maybe they even personalize it, criticizing *you* when they are actually talking about *your work.* They might say that *you* are unclear or inaccurate. Maybe they even say it harshly.

You need to sort out the judgments, separating out the harshness or the over-generalization on the speaker's part. You are left with feedback about your critical thinking on this occasion. Many people view such feedback as negative, but you don't have to view it that way. You can instead view it as a source of valuable information. If you can distance yourself from the negativity, you can free yourself to look for the kernel of truth it may contain.

First, it should be clear to you that you are free to accept or reject people's judgments about you or your work. That's not a moral statement, it's a simple statement of fact. That is not saying that it's right or wrong to do so. It's saying that you *can.* It is within your ability. That includes your teacher's judgments about you. In fact, you already do this.

Because the judgment is not binding on you, you can choose what to learn from it. You may learn something about the other person ("My teacher values grammar very highly. Just how important is grammar?"); but you may also learn something about your work and the way you think ("Well, the fellow student who is responding to my answer says this is irrelevant. Maybe I need to explore this. *Was* my mind drifting to something else? Did I imagine a connection that isn't really there? Or did I not state the connection as clearly as I needed to?").

Critical Thinking and Emotions

CRITICAL THINKING IS NOT EMOTIONLESS THINKING. One of the most widespread myths about critical thinking, and one of the most harmful too, is that critical thinking is somehow opposed to emotions. According to this myth, the best way to think critically is to be devoid of emotions or, if emotions arise, to put them aside, don't let them influence any conclusions drawn. The image is of Mr. Spock on the old *Star Trek* series, putting aside whatever feelings he has, in order to be what he calls "logical."

This is one of the most misleading myths there is, and it is all the more damaging because there is a grain of truth in it. *Some* emotions do indeed get in the way of critical thinking: rage and panic, for example. It is extremely difficult for people to think clearly about a decision when they are enraged. Often, the only reasonable thing they can do in such circumstances is to put off action until the rage subsides, maybe helping it to subside by exercising, or by deep breathing, or by not letting the same enraging thoughts keep repeating in their head.

So, some emotions can interfere with critical thinking. On the other hand, certain other emotion-laden states help with critical thinking: the love of truth is an example. So are the joy of discovery, anger at biased presentations of information, and fear of making an unreasonable decision when something very important hangs in the balance.

Consider as an example something that intrinsically involves a lot of emotion: *love*. Suppose you are the mother of a child. What will help you in being a good mother? A good mother is one who acts in accord with high standards of critical thinking: she has the best interests of her child at heart; she does not neglect her own interests, but she nurtures and makes wise decisions in the best interests of her child, weighs relevant alternative courses of action, and understands the child's strengths and weaknesses, the child's growing need for both autonomy and safety; she is creative about finding ways to help her child develop in a healthy way. Now, what is the role of *love* in this? It should be clear that love—far from being an impediment to clear thinking—is *essential* to being a good critically thinking mother. Love is a large part of what motivates the thinking, grounds it, helps her to assess choices that confront her as a parent. The emotions that go along with love are not in any way opposed to the thinking required to be a good parent.

The same can be said about romantic love. Sometimes it may seem that being in love is opposed to critical thinking, but often this stems from a superficial concept of love. For example, people who are in love often engage in wishful thinking. Suppose Ashley is in love with Lou and Lou is an alcoholic. A common scenario is that Ashley keeps thinking that Lou will be cured any day now, even though it may be clear to others that Lou is not on the road to recovery. But thinking, against all the evidence, that Lou's cure is just around the corner is not an example of *love* interfering with critical thinking. It's deeper than that.

To sort through this example requires thinking through the concept of *love* in a deeper way and distinguishing it from neediness and from a desire to mold the person according to an image. Part of loving someone, romantically or not, is seeing what *that person* is actually like, respecting his or her boundaries. To love someone, rather than just to love an image of that person, is to accept the person as he or she is. Loving the person is exactly what can *help* you see clearly who that person is and your relationship to him or her.

EMOTIONS GIVE US DATA. There is another area in which emotions are essential to critical thinking. Emotions often give us data, and much of the time it's foolhardy to ignore that data. Here's an example of how people often think that love interferes with critical thinking:

A and B, living in Los Angeles, are in love; B decides to accept a lucrative job offer in Chicago; A has been attending school in L.A. Should A quit school and follow B to Chicago?

The example is sometimes used to show that the decision based on love (following B to Chicago) is opposed to the decision based on critical thinking (staying in school in L.A.). But that's not so at all. The best overall decision must be based on such factors as how deep the love is, how long-lasting it is and is likely to remain, the school possibilities in Chicago, and how lucrative the move will be for both A and B. The reasonable decision will be different for different people under different circumstances. That is, the critical-thinking decision might be to follow B to Chicago and go to school there. It is not a critical-thinking decision if A simply *ignores* loving B. If loving B is very important to A, then it's entirely reasonable for that to weigh heavily in A's decision.

In a more general way, though, we receive important data from our emotions all the time. While walking through a neighborhood at dusk, you become afraid that you are in danger. Sometimes people have a narrow view of rationality. If they cannot pinpoint what is dangerous about the situation, they draw the conclusion that their fears are unfounded. But under most circumstances, that's not reasonable at all. There is a good chance that you are picking up clues you are

Describe some situations where, in your best judgment, your emotions led you astray in your reasoning.

Describe some situations where, in your best judgment, your emotions made a positive contribution to your reasoning.

Try to discover patterns in your emotional reactions, so that you can assess when your emotions tend to be accurate responses to reality and when they tend not to be.

For example, think about the people you have been in love with in the past. Have they generally been caring, respectful people who, on the whole, treated you well? If so, that's a pretty good reason to rely on your feelings of love as an indicator of who is good for you: you're pretty good at picking good people. On the other hand, if they were abusive or manipulative, that's a good reason not to put too much weight on your feelings of being in love with someone.

not aware of, triggering your fear. There is nothing unreasonable about heeding that data. On the contrary, what is unreasonable is to pretend that you are not afraid when you are. The reasonable thing to do is neither to ignore the data of your emotions, nor to give them too much weight.

BEING LOGICAL IS LINKED TO HAVING FEELINGS. If we think of desires as intertwined with emotion, then the tie between critical thinking and emotions is even stronger. That is because, in the end, it is not possible to engage in critical thinking without desires and their attendant emotions. Unless I have goals—desires, things I *want*, things I'm emotionally attached to—I have no reason to think critically, no reason to take action X rather than action Y.

Think about Mr. Spock. If Spock acts merely "logically," without paying attention to emotions, why does he bother to save Captain Kirk and the *Enterprise*? Why not let them perish? If he is not emotionally attached to Kirk and the other crew members, he has *no reason* to save them. Unless he *wants* them to live, it is not "logical" for him to save them. Spock's answer is that saving the *Enterprise* is the "right thing to do." But, unless he's emotionally attached to doing the right thing, he has *no reason* to do the right thing. In fact, take any purpose that Spock might give for saving Kirk. The question is always: Why should he try to achieve *that* purpose? It is "logical" for him to try *only if* achieving that purpose is something that matters to him, matters to him in terms of his emotions and desires. Being logical and being reasonable requires having goals that are emotionally important.

The relation between emotions and critical thinking is a complicated one, without easy solutions. (For example, not all philosophers would agree that emotions and desires underlie rationality.) There is no doubt that emotions can cloud judgment, but they can also illuminate it. Fear can make you run from a decision that is in your best interests. But fear can also alert you to dangers in decisions, dangers that you're not consciously aware of. Anger is often a very sophisticated emotion, alerting us to subtle evidence of people's willingness to cross our boundaries. Whether to rely on emotions in any particular case, and how much to rely on them, is itself a matter for critical thinking.

Critical Thinking and Problem Solving

CRITICAL THINKING GOES BEYOND PROBLEM SOLVING. A lot of critical thinking consists of problem solving. You may want to research and figure out the major causes for the amount of violent crime in the United States, or wonder why there are so many earthquakes in California. On a personal level, you may want to improve your study skills or social life. You may map out a scenic route to drive from Denver to Toronto. These are all problems to be solved—or, if "solved" is too strong a word, they are problems to be addressed and figured out as well as possible.

Critical thinking, however, goes beyond problem solving. Some questions or situations are too big or too ill-formed to be classified as problems—still less as problems to be solved. Trying to decide whether to marry X is one of the best examples of a question where critical thinking is essential: for many people there are few other decisions that affect their long-range welfare more than this one. But most of us would not classify a decision about whether to marry someone as "problem solving." Similarly, when a nurse gives a nursing diagnosis for a patient, that's problem solving. But nurses can also think critically about *wellness*: what it means at different age levels, how to promote it in an individual or a community. But wellness is not a *problem*; nor is it a problem to be *solved.*

Another way critical thinking goes beyond problem solving is in the realm of asking questions. Questions are a fundamental part of critical thinking, and one of the most difficult skills in critical thinking is learning to notice that there is a question I should be asking, a problem I should be solving. In problem solving, on the other hand, someone gives me the problem— and my job is to solve it. Critical thinking is different because it begins with posing the problem in the first place.

Find some examples in your textbook or other course material of:

- problems that are meant to be solved

- problems that are meant to be addressed and reasoned through, but not solved

- questions or topics that (like "wellness") are too large to be classified as problems.

Impediments to Critical Thinking

The way we think is an adaptation to the surroundings we have lived in. The patterns in our thinking are ways we have developed to make sense of what goes on around us. These patterns can be effective, but they can also be dysfunctional. Most likely, for each of us, the patterns are variable: effective in some areas, wildly ineffective in others, and mixed most of the time.

Many aspects of the world we live in can be impediments to learning to think more critically.

Forming a Picture of the World on the Basis of the News

Most of us form a picture of what the world is like based on the news: TV news, newspapers, news magazines. Even if you don't watch the news or read newspapers much, you indirectly form a good deal of your picture of the world from the news. You get a picture of what the world is like by talking to friends, or listening to talk shows or MTV, or just through hearsay. But your friends and the people on MTV form *their* picture of the world from the news—and so indirectly you and I do too.

Here is a question I ask my students in Louisiana. (You may not know much about Louisiana, but answer the quiz question anyhow):

> Consider people who are convicted of murder in Louisiana, and sentenced to life imprisonment. How much time do such people, on the average, actually spend in prison? (Remember: the question is not how many years they are sentenced to; it is how many years they end up actually spending in prison):
>
> a. 0–5 years
>
> b. 5–10 years
>
> c. 10–20 years
>
> d. 20–50 years
>
> e. until they die.
>
> Choose an answer before you read on.

I have asked over a thousand students this question over the last five years or so, and only four have ever gotten it right. Even with myself, it was hard to become convinced of the right answer. The first few times I heard it, I simply didn't believe it. (The answer is in the footnotes.[3])

Now, the question in the box is not a critical-thinking question. It is a purely factual question. But there is a critical-thinking question behind our mistaken answer. Where do we get our false impression? We get it, directly or indirectly, from the news media. But how? We do *not* get the wrong answer because the news *tells* us the wrong answer. News media are very careful to check the accuracy of factual statements they report. Rather, what happens is that they report a story about someone getting released from prison early. Maybe over the course of time they report several such stories, including some where a criminal then commits a violent crime while on parole. Maybe we hear politicians or a relative of a victim talking about how prisoners get released early (these people too get their impression from the news). These stories are vivid. They are simplified and made dramatic. Often there is stirring footage. They register in our minds. Whether we are aware of it or not, we form a general picture that violent criminals (including murderers sentenced to life in Louisiana) are getting out of prison early all the time.

Any picture like that one, formed on the basis of news presentations, is likely to be seriously distorted. To see this, answer this question:

What does the news report: what is *usual* or what is *unusual?*

The answer is that news media report on what is *unusual.* That's why it is called *news:* it reports on what is out of the ordinary. That's also why it works so well as entertainment. In contrast, what is

Discuss how likely you are to get a false picture of the following topics from the news:

- the danger of small airplanes
- the amount of crime in your area
- new findings in science
- the chances of winning the lottery

Write down a few important topics of your own where your picture of the world is likely to be seriously distorted if you base your impression mainly on what is reported in the news.

Where, specifically, would you look to get a more accurate impression?

Consider the subject you are studying in this course. Are there topics related to that subject that appear from time to time in the news? If so, is the picture you received from the media likely to be distorted? In what ways? Again, where specifically would you look to get a more accurate picture?

usual is for people to wake up in the morning, eat breakfast, go to work, eat lunch, come home at the end of the day, watch TV for a while, go to bed. That is not a news event. Rather, what the news reports on is Bosnia (hardly a typical country), a fire in an apartment complex (not a common event), an ax-murder in Montana (maybe the only one to occur there in 50 years), a highly controversial bill in Congress (not the hundreds of bills that are passed on a regular basis).

If you want an accurate picture of what the world is *usually* like, you need to look to reputable books, studies, or web sites that deal with the subject in depth. Textbooks are usually an excellent source. And, of course, you have to do some intensive critical thinking about the topic as well.

This doesn't imply that it's wrong to consult the news media regularly. On the contrary, the news—especially if it has more in-depth coverage—is an excellent way to keep up with the unusual, even earthshaking, events of our time.

Forming a Picture of the World on the Basis of Movies, TV, Advertising, Magazines

If forming a picture of the world on the basis of the news results in distortion, forming a picture on the basis of fictionalized or sensationalized material results in vastly more distortion. Sometimes the distortion is obvious, at least to reflective adults: people do not get thrown through plate-glass windows and emerge intact; there is no reason to believe that there are aliens among us; the clothes in the glossy picture will not make most of us look like the model in the picture; products may have unmentioned defects. Other examples are more subtle and affect our attitudes in deep and disturbing ways: trying your hardest, though it may give you personal satisfaction, will not usually result in beating the competition (especially since they may be trying their hardest too); most people's grades (or height or intelligence or abilities) *cannot* be above average; everyone cannot be glamorous, young, physically attractive, or strong; being a lone-wolf rebel who can't get along with superiors does not usually bring success.

List some of the subtle messages acquired from movies, TV, magazines, or advertising that tend to give people a false sense of what the world is like. Then give some that have given *you* a distorted sense of what the world is like.

All-or-Nothing Thinking (Black-and-White Thinking), Us-Versus-Them Thinking, Stereotyping

Each of these ways of thinking is deeply ingrained in us. Some biologists even think we have a built-in genetic bias in favor of thinking in these ways. Nevertheless, each stands in the way of critical thinking, and for similar reasons. Thinking in terms of concepts like these is a way of simplifying our world. In fact, each of them vastly *oversimplifies* the complexity of reality, and each serves as an excuse for *not* thinking things through.

Effective thinking requires us to pay attention to the complexity of things. It requires us to develop a tolerance for ambiguity and an acceptance of less-than-certain answers. It requires a commitment to seeing both sides of an issue and to trying to find out the truth, rather than merely trying to bolster *our* side: our country, our race, our gender, our political views.

Describe a situation from your own life where you engaged in all-or-nothing thinking.

Then describe a contrasting situation, one where you were tempted to engage in all-or-nothing thinking, but instead addressed the subtleties of the situation and therefore came up with a more careful answer.

Describe a similar pair of contrasting examples for us-versus-them thinking, then for stereotyping.

Fears

Although, as we have seen, all fears are not automatically an impediment to critical thinking, some fears do tend to become obstacles. That's especially true of

- fear of making mistakes
- fear of trying something new, of sticking your neck out
- fear of looking foolish

The full exercise of critical thinking requires that you develop intellectual courage. For example, making mistakes is an essential part of critical thinking. What important skill have you ever learned that did not involve making many mistakes? Most critical thinking experts believe that you learn a great deal more from mistakes than from successes. In fact, though you may make fewer critical-thinking mistakes as your higher-order thinking skills develop, there will always be mistakes to be made and learned from.

The same will be true when you try new ways of thinking, when you risk looking foolish by exposing how you think about issues, and when you stick your neck out by giving original solutions to old problems.

Some Educational Practices Discourage Critical Thinking

Some prevalent educational practices discourage critical thinking, and internalizing them as a model of what education should be can seriously affect your critical thinking.

- The student's role is to be a passive recipient of knowledge.
- The student's role is to memorize and regurgitate information.
- The teacher's role is to dispense knowledge.
- Problems assigned to students should always be clearly formulated.
- There is an adequate answer to every question.
- Everything is just a matter of opinion.

How much of your past education has emphasized teacher or student roles such as those listed above?

Formulate your idea of what education should be about, your philosophy of education.

Make some well-considered judgments about how the roles listed fit in with or oppose your idea of education.

Deeper, More Pervasive Impediments to Critical Thinking

In addition to the specific impediments listed previously, there are other deeper and more pervasive obstacles to critical thinking. Four of them are briefly discussed below, but they are not separate from one another. All four are deeply interwoven. Not only that, but they are the kinds of impediments that are very difficult to come to terms with. Maybe it is fair to say that none of us ever completely overcomes them. We can, however, gain deeper insights into how they work, and that can help us overcome their influence.

Egocentrism

Each of us is at the center of our own experience. We live in the middle of our feelings, pains, and pleasures, the things we want and the things we are afraid of, the experiences that have shaped our lives and our attitudes, whether we know it or not. Our experience is heavily influenced by how we think and, conversely, how we think is influenced by our experience.

In accord with this, people often have a way of thinking that always puts themselves first. When I am engaged in such egocentric thinking, I tend to make judgments about how things are, but I may base those judgments on how I wish things to be, or on the basis of how much they agree with my self-interest. This occurs in all of us, probably a good deal of the time. Sometimes it's so blatant that, when it is pointed out to us, we easily see it. Most of the time, though, it operates far beneath the surface. It is easy to delude myself into believing that I am working in the best interests of humanity as a whole when in fact I am working for my own interests and even against the interests of humanity. This is always easier to see in other people than it is in myself.

Egocentrism interferes with critical thinking on all levels, from the deepest to the most superficial. It stands in the way of the empathy that is such an important part of critical thinking. If I am in the health-care professions, for example, it's easy to stay bound up in my own desires and needs and not see things from the patient's point of view. Egocentrism stands in the way of fairmindedness too, another essential component of critical thinking. Part of thinking effectively is being able to understand points of view that are opposed to my own. Sometimes when I feel threatened though, I can't even *hear* what the other person is saying. For many people, when someone critiques their country or culture or religion or family, all they hear is the *fact* that they are being criticized. Anger rises, and often they

The next time someone gets angry at you for some substantive remark you have made, and you didn't expect an angry reaction at all, ask them, "I hear that you're angry at me about my remark. What do you understand me to have said?"

Most of the time, the person will have *mis*understood what you said. Often they will realize this immediately and they'll reply, "Oh. Maybe I didn't hear you right. What *did* you say?"

Write a brief response to the following questions (your response can be just a few lines, but it is important that it be written):

1. **Advertising.** In your judgment, how heavily are people influenced by advertising?

2. **Conformity.** In your judgment, to what extent do people conform to roles dictated by the society they live in?

3. **Driving.** In your judgment, are people generally good drivers?

Write your responses before you look at the answers (see Exercise 1.3 at the end of the chapter).

can't even repeat the substance of the comments the person made. This interferes with their ability to give a fair evaluation of their country, culture, and so on. If I can't hear a critique, then I can't come to a balanced conclusion, and that deprives me of information I can use to assess the validity of my beliefs.

Egocentrism makes it difficult for me to tell accurate from inaccurate statements, it leads me to misunderstand other people's motives as well as my own, it influences me to put incorrect interpretations on what they say.

In course work, egocentrism can lead to my seeing education only in terms of grades, in effect causing me to miss out on all the other benefits to be derived from education. It can lead to plagiarism and cheating, or thinking that teachers are unfair even if they're not.

One of the most valuable things to be gained from critical thinking is an ability to see the egocentricity of our own thinking.

Developmental Patterns of Thinking

We acquire many of our patterns of thinking as we go through different stages of psychological and physical development. As children, we have a number of deeply felt needs: a need to feel safe, a need to be loved, a need for physical contact; we have a need to individuate ourselves from others as well as a contrary need to join completely with another person. Moreover, many of our standard ways of thinking were acquired during childhood, even during early childhood. After all, that's when we first learned how to conceptualize and deal with emotions, frustration, authority figures, strong desires, pain and hurt. Many of the strategies we devised for dealing with these persist, beneath the surface, throughout our lives. Thus, when we feel threatened, we can easily revert back to a child's way of thinking. Problems that can be solved may seem overwhelming. (Think of how overwhelming problems can be to a child.) People can be going about their business with no reference to us at all, and we may feel victimized by it (e.g., waiters who don't see us at their table; drivers who go slow in the left lane; customers who have 20 items in the 15-item checkout lane). We might resort to manipulation or even physical bullying when we don't get our way. Psychologically, that makes sense from a child's relatively helpless point of view.

Those are reversions to childhood. But our thinking can also revert to early adolescence. That's especially true of our judgments about love, romance, and sexuality.

Both childhood and early adolescence, though, are very confusing times, when our critical thinking abilities have not yet developed very much. If we continue to use those patterns of thinking, especially at important junctures in our lives, we can easily perpetuate

Think about the need to feel safe. This is a need that develops in early childhood and never really goes away.

Begin by focusing on other people. Use obvious examples of persistent irrational behavior in people you know: maybe they are abrasive and drive friends away; maybe they identify with groups or with causes that don't seem to serve their interests; maybe they continue to hold beliefs when the vast preponderance of evidence goes against those beliefs; maybe they shout or pout when things don't go their way. Now try out the hypothesis that this behavior is partly the result of looking for feelings of safety along paths established during childhood. (If I drive people away, for example, it can feel as though I don't have to take the risk of depending on them; identifying with groups can give me a feeling of belonging, of safety.)

A much harder exercise is to apply this not just to others, but also to yourself.

(This is not a suggestion to psychoanalyze everyone. It is only a suggestion to examine how much an underlying need to feel safe can be an impediment to critical thinking.)

the situations of the past. So, another great benefit of learning to think critically is that you can start identifying the *assumptions* you used to make about life, and you can distinguish them from the more mature assumptions you can make now. You can separate your past from your present *purposes*. You can take seriously the much more extensive *information* you have now, the *context* in which you now live, the *alternatives* that are now available to you that were not available when you were younger. You can draw different *conclusions*. (The italicized terms are essential critical thinking concepts, elements of reasoning; see Chapter 3.)

Previous Commitments, Previous Personal Experience

Suppose someone makes a point about a controversial issue, about politics maybe, or capital punishment, or the benefits of a trade agreement. The most usual way to evaluate the person's statement is first to see how much it agrees with my views, and then give reasons for or against it based on the degree of agreement.

There is a sense in which this is reasonable, especially if my views are the product of extensive critical examination on my part. But often my views are ones I just happen to hold; they just *seem* to be the result of previous examination. So when I reject a new view because it doesn't agree with the views I already hold, the bias is that it *presumes* that my previously held beliefs are more likely to be correct than the newer points I am evaluating for the first time.

We can also think in a biased way with respect to *evidence*. If I lean toward a certain belief, then just a small amount of evidence weighs heavily in its favor for me. If I believe in aliens visiting earth, or herbal remedies for cancer, or homeopathic cures, or predestination, then even the negative fact that such views have not been absolutely disproven counts heavily in their favor in my eyes.

On the other hand, if I oppose a belief, then a vague piece of evidence, or just the fact that it has not been absolutely proven, weighs heavily against it:

"I don't believe in global warming. Nobody has *proved* the earth is getting warmer."

"Smoking does not cause lung cancer: correlation is not the same thing as causation."

"You can't prove that I won't win the lottery. There's always a chance. You can't win if you don't play."

That is, we slant the amount of evidence to fit in with our predispositions. We require a *mountain* of evidence to make us doubt something we already believe, but we require only the *slightest* of evidence to make us more sure of it.

How *should* we make judgments? If we are interested in accuracy, in knowing the truth or what is likely to come closest to the truth, we should go with the *preponderance of evidence*, regardless of whether we started out for or against a particular conclusion. That is often extremely difficult to do because decisions can be made below the level of our awareness and because our beliefs are so often bound up with our egos and developmental ways of thinking. We can increase our awareness and open-mindedness by using critical thinking.

This is also true when we are basing judgments on *personal experience*. Personal experience gives us a valuable supply of information, one that we can use to draw conclusions, make decisions. One of the main ways teachers get students to think critically about a discipline is by asking them to relate the discipline's concepts to their personal experiences. No one would deny the value of personal experience in critical thinking.

However, personal experience can also be an impediment to critical thinking. That's particularly true of vivid personal experiences, the kind that are unusual and imprint themselves on our minds. For each of us, our personal experience is limited. If we make generalizations from it that go beyond what we are acquainted with, we stand a good chance of drawing distorted conclusions. Your own experience has far more impact on you than the experiences of a hundred other people you hear about. That is true, but if you want to draw accurate conclusions about what is likely to happen, then (other things being equal) you should put more faith in the experiences of a hundred people than in the experience of one—even if that one happens to be you.

What do you need to do to broaden your knowledge base so as to take account of a wide variety of experiences and conclusions beyond your own? You should look at reputable books, studies, journal articles, sources that gather and assemble information from a great variety of human experience. If you own a Toyota that repeatedly gives you trouble, that is an excellent reason not to trust that car in the future. But if you want to make a wise decision about whether the next car you buy should be a Toyota, your personal experience is too limited. It would be wiser to consult *Consumer Reports* or some other neutral agency that evaluates cars. The best-selling and highly influential *Men Are from Mars, Women Are from Venus* draws conclusions about what men and women are really like—but the conclusions are based on the behavior of only a handful of American men and women who decided to go into therapy and consulted the author. That sample is so tiny and unrepresentative that when it is projected on to men and women in general, it's liable either to be inaccurate or to be seen as accurate only because it's a set of stereotypes. What should the author have done if he wanted to think critically about profound differences between men and women? At the very least, he needed to consult well-substantiated studies of men and women from a great variety of cultures, and he needed to research the behavior of people who have never consulted a therapist.

How Deep Is Our Need for Critical Thinking?

One of the great things about critical thinking is its versatility. It is valuable at all levels of our thinking.

At the Level of Practical Decision Making

Critical thinking helps when we are simply trying to deal with ordinary tasks: how to study more efficiently, find a strategy when we are stuck in an airport, decide what kind of clothes to buy. This is thinking about the means to use to accomplish a goal. It is problem solving of the most authentic kind. This is an important level of critical thinking, one that addresses all those ordinary decisions we make.

Developing thinking skills helps you envision alternative paths you could take. It helps you identify and discard outdated assumptions you may be making. It helps you anticipate some of the consequences, both positive and negative, of decisions you or others may make. It helps you keep your goals in sight and think of more effective means of achieving those goals.

At the Level of Meaningfulness

Learning to think critically also helps people deal with the much larger issues of living their life. Critical thinking frees people, the way nothing else really can, from habits of thinking they are often ruled by. Not completely of course, but substantially. Critical thinking opens up other viable courses of action that leave people far more fulfilled, paths that otherwise might never occur to them. Finding a life partner or a new occupation, incorporating the profound knowledge that's available in your courses into your way of thinking about your life, developing reasonable attitudes toward self, toward others, toward your values, toward all the things that make life meaningful for you—all of these can be made richer and more attainable by examining them thoughtfully.

At the Level of Concepts

We think in terms of *concepts,* and these inevitably shape our life to a considerable degree. Very often the concepts we think in terms of are ones we accept uncritically. We may understand what love is from movies and from the way we feel. We may understand what freedom is simply by having heard the word over and over and making vague associations with it. We may grow up thinking justice means getting even. We all have concepts of what it is to be a student, a teacher, a woman, a man, a religious person, an atheist, a scientist, an artist, a professional in the field we are studying. We have concepts of what it means to be brave, to be treated fairly, to be intelligent, to be cool, to be anything you can name or describe. We can reach a deep level of critical thinking by examining our concepts critically, becoming more aware of the way individual concepts help us or hurt us, limit us or free us.

Even aspects of ourselves that are distinct from thinking are heavily influenced by our concepts. Desires, for instance: If you like something, or hate it—a person, a movie, a subject in school, a kind of car—the liking or the hating is not itself an instance of thinking. Rather, the liking or hating is influenced by the concepts you use in

Many people automatically assume that bravery is good. But here are some possible examples where bravery makes a situation worse, where being brave does damage:

- someone who is brave but a Nazi
- a sports figure who bravely plays despite a serious injury
- prisoners who are brave in defiance of the system and even of self-interest
- Achilles, the hero of *The Iliad.* Did his bravery accomplish what you would call worthwhile purposes?

Plato would say that these examples are not part of the concept of bravery at all. How might someone believe that?

In your view, are these examples of bravery, or of something else? Why? If they are examples of bravery, would you admire the action in each case?

your thinking. It is only recently that anyone thought suntans were beautiful, that beaches were a desirable place to spend a vacation, that thinness in men and women was attractive, that wilderness held value, that toleration was a virtue, that democracy was workable, that it was unhealthy to be a caretaker in a relationship. Our standard concepts for each of these key terms has changed, become strikingly more positive or negative. The concepts may well change again. It can be liberating to step out of the fads that come and go with respect to what is desirable. Re-examining the concepts you have of the things you desire will help you rise above the fads.

Similarly, although emotions are not the same as thoughts, they are closely linked. Being afraid or being joyful is, in itself, not an example of thinking. But, again, your concepts have an immense influence on *what* you are afraid of and *what* brings you joy. If you are afraid of the dark, afraid of math, or even afraid of dying—these are not universal fears. There are many people, not very different from you, who don't share these fears. Some people feel safe in the dark, delight in math (even if they are not very good at it), and find peace and acceptance in contemplating death. We fear things in part because of the *concepts* we have of those things, because of how we classify them and think about them.

The influence of our thinking extends even to bodily sensations: "Even though nerve signals work the same way, something as obviously biological as pain in childbirth is experienced differently depending on cultural expectations [that is, on concepts in our culture]. Women develop expectations not just about how they should respond but about how they should experience their own sensations and emotions."[4]

Emotions are not really under our direct control, though how we act on those emotions often is. Many of the ways people try to gain direct control over their emotions actually hurt. If you are afraid of speaking in public, for example, but feel you shouldn't be afraid of it, you can try to suppress the fear. Maybe you can even force yourself to speak in public, or pretend to yourself that you are not afraid of it. You can reason as follows: "It doesn't make sense to feel fearful of speaking in public. There's really nothing to be afraid of. Therefore, I am not afraid of speaking in public." This is called denial. *Denial* is when you keep yourself from seeing something you know is true. The classic case is alcoholics who refuse to see that they are alcoholics. Many people confuse denial of this sort with being rational. Neither suppression nor denial is very healthy. Neither is very effective either, at least not in the long run. Both have high psychological costs.

Though our emotions are not under our direct control, they can be indirectly affected by addressing our concepts. You can work on your concept of public speaking and try to understand why you see it as fearsome. You can admit and honor the fear that arises. You can investigate what its roots are, what associations you have with it that generate the fear, and build new associations. You can rethink the concept over time, and usually this will be effective in changing your reaction to it.

The Experience of Learning to Think Things Through

You may already be good at thinking critically. In some areas you may be very good at it. In fact, in some areas you may be so good at critical thinking that it occurs naturally—you no longer even recognize it as good thinking. For example, you are driving down a street and a ball bounces out in front of you from between parked cars. You *instinctively* put your foot on the brake; you *instinctively* look around, searching for the child who might dart out. Another example: there's a sudden accident in the cars ahead of you. To get out of the way, you *instinctively* pull to the right rather than to the left.

These *seem* instinctive, but they're not. You've *learned* to do these things, and you haven't learned them as a conditioned reflex. You've learned them by reflection on likely consequences. You've internalized the critical thinking so well that it seems natural, instinctive. But these actions are still the product of critical thinking.

For most people, it is difficult to learn a new skill from a book. Think of learning how to drive a car, or dance ballet, or write. To acquire skills like these from scratch, it may be essential to have feedback: "Is this the way to parallel park?" "Should I position my feet like this?"

But critical thinking is not that way, at least not entirely. You already have a lot of critical thinking skills. It is an activity you already engage in, probably to a significant degree. For skills you already have, reading a book can improve them dramatically. If you're able to write, drive, and dance, you can improve those skills by reading books that guide you through techniques. Of course, it's not enough *just* to read the book. You have to try it out, act on it, put it into practice. You have to *do* the writing, driving, dancing, *do* the critical thinking.

In fact, you can be confident that if you work your way through this book, your thinking skills will improve significantly. That is so because of the reflectiveness critical thinking requires. By working through this book, you will become more reflective, more aware of the dimensions of your thinking, and the skills will improve.

The trouble is, you may not *feel* as if your skills are improving. The improvement is unlikely to be obvious. Many people have the opposite reaction. They feel they are getting *worse* at reasoning as they work through a course that emphasizes critical thinking.

That happens for a number of reasons. First, working through a disciplined process of critical thinking will slow your thinking down. A problem that you once effortlessly thought your way through will now take much longer. You will have to focus on all the parts of the thinking that you previously took for granted.

Second, questions will start to arise for you where none arose before. "Am I being clear?" "Is this really an implication?" "Maybe I'm jumping to a conclusion here." "How can I check up on this?" Questions are a sign of growth, of opening to new ways of thinking. But we often believe that questions are a sign of *not* understanding, that it is better to have no questions at all. Critical thinking lives in questions.

Third, the reflectiveness of critical thinking can cause you to start second-guessing yourself, especially at the beginning, or when you are feeling down on yourself. Before, you might have confidently asserted an answer; now, however, you might reflect, "Wait a minute, maybe I'm jumping to a conclusion here," or: "Is this really an implication of this author's position? Maybe I'm being unduly influenced by the fact that I disagree with her."

Fourth, some of your certainty about things can be a bluff to cover up the threatening fact that you really don't know, or don't know for sure. The main person you are bluffing may be yourself. Studying how to think critically often calls your bluff. You start asking, "What assumptions does my automatic response rest on?" Answers you might have given before with utter certainty now seem much shakier.

Finally, as Michael Scriven explained in a classic text on reasoning, if you are a swimmer or a tennis player and you start studying with a professional coach, you'll find that you have to change many of the ways you do things, unlearning certain moves and learning others. This will feel awkward, and it will slow you down—at first. But that slowing down is really the only way to build up proficiency and reliable speed. "Speed builds slowly."[5]

Here is a list of reactions many people have to studying critical thinking. You should not be surprised, or troubled, by experiencing many of them. (In fact, as a teacher I would be troubled if you experienced *none* of them.)

- difficulty applying critical thinking terms in practice
- not being able to tell if you have applied them correctly
- becoming overly concerned with how one concept overlaps with another
- becoming confused about things that seemed clear before

- persistently doubting that you will ever improve
- initial confidence in an answer, followed by nagging doubt
- a feeling that you knew the discipline a lot better before you had to think critically about it
- a feeling that your teachers are not knowledgeable enough because they generate more questions than answers

When trying to learn to think critically from a book, what's important is to engage in the *activities* of critical thinking, not just *read about* them. Unfortunately, many people have a model of thinking that does them disservice. They conceive of thinking as a solitary activity, something you do in the privacy of your own head.

But one of the best ways to learn to think things through, especially in a discipline, is with cooperative learning. Critical thinking is best when it is not done in a vacuum. It helps to have the give and take of discussion, to receive feedback on your thinking, to weigh other viewpoints, other approaches.

Here is a simple critical-thinking template, which can be applied in any area where you and others are trying to think things through.

CRITICAL THINKING TEMPLATE

- Find four or five other people who are also trying to think critically about this area. (This can be done in person, via e-mail, or in chat groups.)
- Figure out the three most central organizing concepts or ideas that underlie the area. (For example, the three main concepts in a chapter you are studying for this course.)
- Begin with some pre-writing. Take the time to write a paragraph or so to explain how those concepts operate in the world, in your life, or in the subject matter. The explanations should be in your own words—not in the words of the teacher or the text. Examples you give should be from your own understanding, not examples given previously by teachers, texts, or other students. When all of you are done, take turns giving your explanation of these major concepts to the other people in the group. You can say them to one another or, better, you can duplicate them so everyone has a copy. The writing may be just jotting things down, but it is important that your responses be *written*. Written responses are concrete and allow you to confront your thoughts in black and white.
- Group members critique the explanation given. (Remember that critiquing is not the same as criticizing or finding fault.) In the critique,

→ focus on the elements from Chapter 3. Did the writer specify the *purpose* behind the concepts? Identify key *assumptions?* Look for *consequences,* for *alternatives?* and so on.

→ focus on the standards from Chapter 4. Was the explanation *clear?* Was it *accurate?* Did it explain what was most *important?* and so on.

An Overview of the Book that Lies Ahead

Here is the basic model of this text, in a nutshell.

When people engage in critical thinking, they start off with some question. They try to answer it by reasoning their way through it.

1. There are elements of reasoning. The elements are the basic building blocks of reasoning or thinking. *Assumption* is an element. When people reason things out, they make assumptions. So one way to examine their reasoning is to focus on that element of their reasoning: *assumption.* We can ask, "What assumptions are they making?" (The elements are explained in Chapter 3.)

So if the question is Q, we can picture the reasoning process thus far as shown in Figure 1.1.

FIGURE 1.1   *The process of reasoning.*

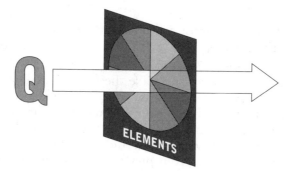

2. There are also standards of reasoning. They can also be called "standards of critical thinking." These standards determine whether people are reasoning through the question *well* or not. *Accuracy* is an example of a standard. So one way to examine how well they have reasoned it out is to focus on that standard of reasoning: *accuracy.* We can ask, "Are the assumptions they have made accurate?" (The standards are explained in Chapter 4.)

You can picture the standards as a set of filters (see Figure 1.2). They are used to filter out reasoning that doesn't meet the standards.

FIGURE 1.2 *The process of critical thinking: reasoning through the elements and standards.*

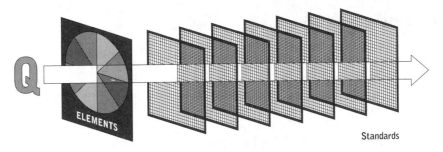

3. **Suppose the question being addressed is one related to the discipline or field you are studying.** Maybe it is a question your teacher has assigned; maybe it's from the textbook in the subject; maybe it's your own question.

There are ways of thinking that lie at the heart of the discipline you are studying. These include fundamental and powerful concepts, and central questions of the discipline. Disciplines are not bits and pieces; they are not assemblages of facts. Instead, there is a logic to thinking in that discipline. For example, if the course you are taking is in sociology, then that logic, taken all together, constitutes the way a sociologist thinks. In biology, the goal is to think biologically, to think the way a biologist thinks. In history, the goal is to think historically.

The concepts will differ from field to field. *Social patterns* is an example of a fundamental and powerful concept in sociology. So one way to examine how well people have reasoned out a question in the discipline of sociology is to focus on that fundamental and powerful concept: *social patterns.* We can ask, "Have they drawn conclusions, accurate conclusions, in terms of what we know about social patterns?" (Critical thinking in a discipline is explained in Chapter 2.)

You can picture the discipline as a lens or set of lenses through which people reason. Figure 1.3 gives us a full picture.

FIGURE 1.3 *The process of critical thinking in a discipline.*

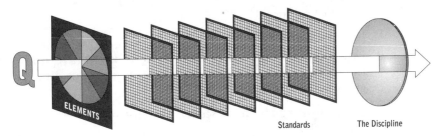

Some of the questions in this and later chapters call for the straightforward application of concepts from the text, but some are more than that. Some ask you to *extend* concepts in the text to new areas and then to think critically about these extensions. Some of the exercises are designed to teach new concepts. Answering them *is* part of learning to think critically.

Exercises with a star (✷) behind the numbers are ones that have answers (or at least responses) at the back of the book. The responses there are not necessarily complete. Sometimes they are very sketchy. Often they simply point out one dimension it would be wise to consider when answering the question. Sometimes the starred response will contain additional questions as well.

1.1 What are some "good questions" you have about this course? Ask some good questions in each sense (ones that open up central areas and ones that you really want to know the answer to). What are some "bad questions" you could raise about the course (bad in the sense of superficial or bad in the sense that you don't really care about the answer)?

1.2 Thinking versus reflective thinking. You'll notice that many of the exercises in this book ask you to *reflect*: on aspects of the discipline you are studying, on your life, on your experiences in school, on your relation to the subject matter you are learning.

Here is an example:

A. What should I do about this patient?

B. What should I do about this patient, keeping in mind that the purpose of this treatment is X?

In B, focusing on *purpose* helps make the thinking more reflective.

Another example:

A. How should I study for my final exams?

B. How should I study for my final exams, keeping in mind the consequences (both positive and negative) of different ways of studying?

In B, thinking about *consequences* helps make the thinking more reflective.

Write down three questions that you think about often. At least one should focus on the means to achieve a certain end. Then, formulate the questions *reflectively*, using the concept of *purpose, consequences, assumptions,* or *alternatives.*

1.3 Go back to the box on p. 28 and look at the responses you gave about advertising, conformity, and driving.

Now turn the question to *yourself*: To what extent are *you* influenced by advertising? To what extent do *you* conform to roles dictated by society. Are you a better-than-average driver?

1.4 Raising central questions. Here are some "facts" or alleged facts. Formulate good questions about each. Explain why each is a good question.

a. The U.S. is #1.

b. Ninety-eight percent of the genetic material in humans and chimpanzees is identical.

c. "A child's drawing that expresses some feeling about mother, father and home is as much an artwork as Michelangelo's . . . Sistine Chapel frescoes."[6]

d. Smoking causes more deaths per year in the U.S. than alcohol, illegal drugs, murder, suicide, and AIDS all together.

e. "On Christmas Day 1991 a weary and bitter Gorbachev resigned as president of the USSR and recognized The Commonwealth of Independent States. The Soviet Union had dissolved."[7]

1.5 Review the definition of *denial* and the examples given there. (Here's another standard example: Smokers who deny that smoking causes early death.)

Identify three of your own examples of denial (they can be from your own life or someone else's). Explain how denial can appear "rational" to the person engaged in it.

1.6 A woman goes for a haircut at a national hair-cutting chain. The hairdresser asks her what brand of shampoo she uses. He then puts some of her hairs under a microscope and shows her that there is a white film on the hairs. He recommends that she buy the store's brand of shampoo rather than the one she has been using.

What would be some good questions for her to ask herself about this situation?

1.7 Group activity. Individually write out some other factors that you see as impediments to developing your own critical-thinking skills. Then, prioritize the list, choosing that factor that is the greatest impediment for you.

Sit in groups of four. Person A begins, explaining how that factor is an impediment for him or her. Proceed through person B, C, and D in the same way.

Discuss the extent to which all four share the same impediments.

Then, the whole group should focus on Person A's impediment. Together, try to devise a practical strategy to counteract some of the influence that impediment has on critical thinking. Do the same for each group member.

1.8 Envision a prospective employer who might hire you after graduation. What are the most important understandings he or she would want you to have learned from your college education? How does this relate to critical thinking?

 1.9 On p. 2, you described a situation in which you thought through something critically, and another in which you did not think through something critically.

For each, what *criteria* did you use to decide? That is, what earmarks of the first situation told you that it was an example of good thinking? And what earmarks of the second situation told you that you did not think it through critically?

1.10 Name three things you have seen in movies that tend to give people a distorted view of the world. Discuss how they are misleading. Give an example of each.

Now, name three things you have seen in movies that have been seriously misleading for *you*. Explain briefly how they were misleading.

1.11 Give an example of a situation where your emotions led you in the wrong direction. Then give an example of a situation where your emotions led you in the right direction. In terms of critical thinking, how do you explain the difference?

1.12 It is one of those days when people seem to be driving erratically. Far more than usual, people are cutting you off, slamming on their brakes unexpectedly, or driving too slow.

What are some good hypotheses to explain the way people are driving?

1.13 You may notice some features of this book as you read. One is that it tends to use qualifier words a great deal; another is that it sometimes uses "I" in examples rather than "you" (e.g., on p. 11).

Using qualifier words is a conscious effort to avoid all-or-nothing thinking. Qualifier words are ones like *often, almost always, tends to, usually, virtually.* The general principle is that people are justified in making an all-or-nothing statement only if they have good enough reasons to back it up. As a critical thinker, I am often personally offended by a bald statement like "Power corrupts, and absolute power corrupts absolutely."[8] We are entitled to make that strong a claim only if we have good reason—not just a hunch or an impression—that power automatically corrupts people.

Read through a page of your text in the discipline. Circle all the qualifier words you find there. Explain why the author used the qualifier word instead of saying the sentence in a more absolute way. Next identify claims that could have contained qualifier words, but don't. Explain why the author said it this way.

On p. 11 can you see why the text uses "I" rather than "you"?

Are there other aspects of the way this text is written that seem to you unusual? Can you see any of them as responses to aspects of critical thinking?

1.14 Here is a professor of education interviewing a student, a prospective elementary school teacher, about a class the student has just taught. The student was teaching that there should be equality between the sexes.

> Professor: What if the parents came into the class and said, "We don't want you teaching that to our son." What would you say to them?

> Student: I would ask them why they feel that way, listen to their concerns. I would explain the situation in terms of how I feel about it . . .

> Professor: How would you justify your position to them?[9]

    a. In terms of critical thinking, what is the difference between the two ways the professor asked his question? That is, what is the difference between asking "What would you say to them?" and "How would you justify your position to them?"

    b. How *would you* justify teaching that there should be equality between the sexes?

1.15 The topic of Chapter 3 is the elements of reasoning. Three of those elements are *conclusions, assumptions,* and *points of view.* Think of a difficult situation in your life, a problem in your relationship with someone, a decision you have to make, or something important about this course.

Formulate three good questions about that situation, one using each of the three elements listed. Then answer the questions, as well as you can.

1.16 **Work in pairs.** Each person chooses one written answer to an exercise in this chapter. (Alternatively, you could choose a written answer you gave to a critical thinking problem about the discipline.)

Exchange papers with the person next to you. Each of you then writes comments on the *reasoning* in the other person's paper. Return the papers.

What can you learn about your paper from what the other person has said? What can you learn about what the other person values?

1.17 **Group work.** Use the template on pp. 37–38 to address the topic of critical thinking as you understand it so far.

- Gather with four or five people to critically discuss the topic.

- In a discussion, figure out the three most central organizing concepts that underlie the conception of critical thinking being presented in this book. Try to come to consensus, but if you can't, you are not required to use the other people's central concepts for the next step. If you believe yours are well thought out, use them.

- Begin with some pre-writing. Write a paragraph or so about how those three concepts work in your life (or in the discipline you are taking). Use your own words; don't stick to the words in this text. Give some of your own examples. When you are done, make duplicates for everyone.

- Each person critiques the responses of the others in the group. Focus on two standards → Was the response clearly stated? (If it is, you can probably come up with your own examples.) → Was it accurate?

What Is Critical Thinking Within a Field or Discipline?

Y ou are studying within a field, discipline, or subject matter. What is it to think critically within that field or discipline or subject? What is it to think critically in biology or math, in physical education, or nursing, or writing? At its heart, critical thinking is the same whether it is within a specific field or about anything else. It is helpful to take two of the definitions of critical thinking from Chapter 1 and apply them to specific fields. For example, apply Robert Ennis's definition to the field of biology:

> Critical thinking in biology is reasonable, reflective biological thinking that is focused on deciding what to believe or do in biology and in the relation between biology and the world at large.

Pre-think what your course will be about. Identify a course you are taking (composition, ballet, elementary education), and write two or three paragraphs on what the course *is*. Try to capture what composition, ballet, or elementary education *is*. What are the goals of the field or subject? What are the main questions that you think will be addressed? How does it fit in with other courses?

Similarly, we can apply Matthew Lipman's definition to the field of history:

> Critical thinking in history is skillful, responsible thinking that is conducive to good historical judgment, because it is sensitive both to historical contexts and to other contexts which have a relation to history; it relies on historical criteria, and it is self-correcting.

The rewritten definitions may be a little cumbersome, but it is worthwhile taking time to ponder what makes thinking in the field you are studying *skillful* or *responsible.* What is involved in being a *reflective* nurse or psychologist? What is it to think in a *reasonable* way in music or political science? What are the main *contexts* a critical-thinking engineer or writer must be sensitive to?

The Parts of Critical Thinking Within a Field

We can also take the three parts of critical thinking discussed in Chapter 1 and apply them to learning a subject. Critical thinking in a field involves asking good questions, reasoning out responses, and believing the results of our reasoning.

Asking the Question

If I am a student thinking critically in a field, I will find myself asking questions in the field. I will be asking questions about the reading, about what I hear from teachers as well as from other students, about the subject matter, and about my own beliefs and understanding. I won't necessarily ask them out loud, and I will not expect them all to be answered, but with practice, and once I start freeing myself from a passive model of what it is to be a student, I will probably be flooded with questions—far more questions than I can answer.

In fact, that is a good rough-and-ready test of whether you are becoming more of a critical thinker in the field. You will see complexities beneath the surface, ones you never noticed before. You'll notice a lot more places where things are not as clear to you as they seemed before. You may find yourself confused in cases when previously you would not have understood enough even to be confused: before, you would simply have taken notes.

To begin, identify the most central ideas in the course—maybe from the name of the course—and ask yourself, "What *are* they?" For instance, "What *is* abnormal psychology?" "On the deepest level I can think at, what makes something abnormal?" "What *is* the purpose of psychology?" In a management course: "What is it to manage an office?" That is a *deep* question, one that you can ask yourself at different points in your life, and come up with differing and deeper answers every time. You cannot be an effective office manager unless you re-answer that question when business conditions change, the office changes, or you yourself change.

In a physics course, you can ask, "How does an object get from point A to point B? How does it *do* it? How do forces work? How

Pick a paragraph in your textbook—one that has a lot of "stuff" in it. Ask yourself some of the following questions:

- What does it mean?

- How can I use that information?

- What implications does it have (beyond any that are mentioned)?

- What evidence does it rest on?

- What reasoning was the content of that paragraph based on?

- Do all the experts in the field see the issue in the same way?

- What are some alternative points of view?

- Though the paragraph may be presented in a clear way, what complications arise?

does energy get transferred?" Don't allow questions like these to be answered simply by definitions the text gives. Definitions are an *aid* to thinking through the question and answer. They are not, by themselves, "the answer."

Richard Feynman, the Nobel laureate in physics, tells a story about when he was a boy. He noticed that the ball in his wagon kept rolling even after he stopped the wagon. He asked his father why that happened. His father gave him a profound answer, one that is rooted in a spirit of asking questions: "The general principle is that things which are moving tend to keep on moving. . . . This tendency is called 'inertia,' but nobody knows why it's true."[1] Feynman points out how the answer, inertia, could have been used to stifle the wonder behind the boy's question. The answer his father gave, on the other hand, promoted further questioning.

It takes practice to improve at critical thinking. That is particularly true of learning to ask questions. If you are like many other students, when you read a paragraph in your text or you listen to a lecture, no questions come up for you at all. As you work on your critical thinking, though, that will change. But you should guard against the idea that having no questions shows that you understand something. For any subject matter that is at all complicated, the opposite is the case: if no questions arise for you, it probably means that you do not understand it deeply enough to see the many paths of questioning that arise.

REASONING IT THROUGH. Reasoning in a field can be difficult. Initially, it requires that you recognize both what you know *and* what you need to know but don't. Additionally, it means being able to draw conclusions on the basis of reasons.

Think of the difference between memorizing a list of the causes of World War I and reasoning those causes out. The historians who first formulated the thesis that WWI came about as a result of entangling alliances *reasoned* this out as an answer, and so do all the people who rethink this answer for themselves. They reexamine how adequate it is, whether it's deep enough as a cause. They amend it, add to it; some of them end up rejecting the idea that entangling alliances were a major cause of WWI. Jennifer Reed, a history professor, regularly asks her students to work through not just a single set of causes of WWI, but also causes that are geographic, political, economic, social, technological, and personal. She helps students reason out what combination of these causes was necessary and sufficient for the event.[2]

That is an example of reasoning in the field of history. It is entirely different—different in *kind*—from merely repeating what someone else said about the causes of WWI. In its fullest sense, reasoning in a field involves being able to use the elements (Chapter 3) and standards (Chapter 4) of critical thinking in the subject matter.

Take a paragraph or two from your text, selected by you or your teacher. The paragraphs may be largely composed of factual material; they may contain reasoned judgments, but in either case, they are the product of *reasoning*. So picture them as *conclusions,* conclusions that people have drawn from a long process of reasoning. Try to describe the process of reasoning that might have led to these conclusions.

The paragraphs may contain:

- a set of definitions or classifications → Can you describe the disorganized state of affairs that existed before these definitions and classifications were formulated?

- factual matters that are the results of tests or investigations (these may not even be mentioned) → Can you determine the kinds of tests and investigations that led to these results?

- biographical or background information → Can you describe the kinds of primary sources that this information is derived from?

BELIEVING THE RESULTS. It may seem that, as you become more adept at asking questions in the field and then reasoning through the answers, you will automatically believe the results of your reasoning. But believing the results of your reasoning—or acting on that reasoning—may not follow.

Here is a personal example. I learned in school that heavy objects and light objects fall toward the earth at the same rate. Everyone learns this. It is a scientific law. And, of course, I know that law is true. I learned it many times in school; if you ask me on an exam, I will give the right answer. But despite all that, I strongly suspect that I don't really believe it! That is, I think that *in my heart* I probably don't believe it: if I had to bet my life on the outcome, without a lot of time to think it over, I'm afraid I might bet that the heavy one would hit the ground first.

Here is another example, a far more serious one. One of the hardest things to teach student nurses and other health-care practitioners to do is to wash their hands between patients. It is easy, however, to get student nurses to *say* they will wash their hands. If you ask on a test, "It is important to wash your hands: TRUE or FALSE," they will always

Give some examples of findings in the field you are studying that you don't believe.

These may fall into two distinct categories. The first is where you straightforwardly *disagree* with claims or positions in the field. You may or may not have any of these. If you do, write some of them down.

The second category is much harder to identify. It is where the findings in the field subtly conflict with background stories or accounts that you already have in your head. (See pp. 69–72.) These background stories may not be fully formulated in your mind; they may not be conscious at all. (My example of heavy versus light objects is an example of this.)

It is especially important to look for this second category as the course progresses. Why is that important? Because if you don't, you won't really be taking the subject matter seriously—and *not* because you disagree, but rather because you have an unexamined story guiding your thoughts. And it may well be a story that you will reject once you have thought about it.

get the right answer. They can also correctly explain why hand-washing is necessary. What's difficult is getting them to learn to *do* it.

In 1996, there was a conference in New Orleans for experts on infectious diseases. These were doctors, not nurses. Some graduate students stationed themselves in the restrooms and counted how many of these doctors washed their hands after using the restroom. They found that 13 percent of the women and 44 percent of the men did not. And these were *experts* in *infectious diseases!*[3] (This does not by itself prove that they would not wash their hands in the hospital—but it does suggest that they have not completely internalized their thinking about the importance of hand-washing.)

Thinking Biologically, Thinking Sociologically, Thinking Philosophically, Thinking Musically . . .

There is another way to describe what it is to think critically in a field or discipline: the discipline works as a set of lenses through which you can see the world in a more focused way. (Look back at

Figure 1.3.) You can picture the discipline's lenses as like the ones inside a microscope or telescope: they let you look more deeply into events or see the distant up close.

Critical thinking in a field is thinking things through *in terms of* the concepts of the field. Critical thinking in biology is *thinking biologically*. Critical thinking in the field of anatomy is *thinking anatomically*. Critical thinking in geography is taking any problem having to do with the spatial ordering of the earth and *thinking it through geographically*. Notice how broad the application of such thinking is: it goes far beyond those problems that are brought up in the course.

Not all fields have a convenient adverb attached to them, such as "biologically." We can't say someone thinks "nursingly" or "marketingly." But we can still use the idea: Critical thinking in nursing is thinking the way an observant, informed, reasonable nurse thinks. Critical thinking in literature is thinking the way a knowledgeable, sensitive, reasonable literary reader thinks.

So what is it to think biologically? Here is an example that gets at it, at least in a negative way. In my critical thinking course, virtually all students have taken a course in biology, either recently or in the past. So for several years I gave a quiz (not for a grade) in which I asked students to define 10 biological terms. I chose ordinary terms, such as *cell*, and some more specialized terms, such as *mitochondria* or *endoplasmic reticulum*. As you might guess, there was a wide divergence in the students' ability to define them: some were able to define many of them and some only a few or none. Students did better defining ordinary terms like *cell* than they did defining terms like *mitochondria*. Keep in mind that the course has nothing to do with biology. Several weeks later I gave another quiz. In this one I asked students to write a paragraph or two in response to some questions like these:

What happens when you cut your finger and get an infection?

How does a person catch sexually transmitted diseases?

What happens when someone gets cancer?

How are babies made?

Why is it harmful to get a suntan?

Students answered these questions in various ways. But in two years of classes, virtually no one ever used the word *cell* in his or her responses. And this was the result *whether or not* they had defined *cell* correctly on the earlier quiz. I conclude from this informal experiment that the term *cell* had not become a significant part of the way these people thought through questions. The concept of cell had not become internalized.

But cell is an important concept. It is different from mitochondria. For most of us who are not professional biologists, we will probably never confront a problem for which thinking in terms of mitochondria will help us make better choices. But that is decidedly not true of cell: cell is a *powerful* concept. Thinking in terms of cells gives insight into how to answer the ordinary questions we confront daily.

You can think biologically at any level of educational expertise, in high school, in college, as a graduate student in biology, as a professional biologist. At each level, though, you need to incorporate the concept of cell into the way you habitually think through questions. You need to apply that concept not just to questions specifically asked in the course, and not just to those that are labeled "biology questions," but to any question about our life processes where the concept of cell will yield insight and promote better choices.

One of the main goals of a biology course is to help you internalize the most central biological concepts and to learn to think through questions in your life using those concepts. That is what it is to think biologically. Similarly, thinking mathematically is, in a way, seeing the world in terms of quantity. Thinking historically is not the same as knowing a hodgepodge of events and persons from the past. Rather, it revolves around a central question: How are events made meaningful by the past they grow out of?

Sarah Blaffer Hrdy is a brilliant evolutionary anthropologist, and her description conveys beautifully what it is to think in terms of that field:

> For better or for worse, I see the world through a different lens than most people. My depth of field is millions of years longer, and the subjects in my viewfinder have the curious habit of spontaneously taking on the attributes of other species: chimps, platypuses, australopithecines. This habit of thinking about mothers in broad evolutionary and comparative—as well as cross-cultural and historical—perspectives distinguishes my examination of motherhood from those of the psychoanalysts, psychologists, novelists, poets, and social historians whose work I build on.[4]

This way of thinking is available not just to professional anthropologists like Hrdy, but to almost anyone. It can open up clear, accurate, important perspectives for the way we conceptualize our lives.

The Logic of the Field or Discipline

What Is a Field or Discipline?

There is, unfortunately, a common impression that a field is essentially a body of information. It is as if geology were equivalent to all the information we have acquired in geology. But that is an inaccurate and misleading view of what a field is. True, geologists, professional or amateur, have a good deal of information. But a field is far more than that. Fields are dynamic: they change, grow, evolve. Fields embody a distinctive way, or set of ways, of looking at the world. The perspective of geology is different from the perspective of geography or sociology or psychology.

Practitioners in a field—at whatever level of education—do not simply possess information. Rather, they know how to use that information as well as the concepts that structure it. They are able to apply both of those to new cases. They know how to synthesize the information. They know how to think *about* the field, and they know how to think *within* the field.

A field or discipline embodies a way of thinking about the world, a way of solving problems and answering questions. A field involves a distinct set of purposes, key assumptions about the world, key concepts and models that people in the field use to interpret and group the information. A good way to describe practitioners is to say that they have ownership of *the logic of* the field.

John Maynard Keynes, a great economist of the twentieth century, said that economics "is a method rather than a doctrine, an apparatus of the mind, a technique which helps its possessor to draw correct conclusions."[5]

A theme of this book is that we can substitute the name of *any* discipline for economics in this quotation, and have an insightful description of that discipline as a way of reasoning.

The Concept of the *Logic of a Field*

Almost everyone has experienced learning *parts* of a subject, but with no idea at all of how those parts fit together. Though this can happen in any field, it is dramatically true of many people's experience of algebra. You can learn how to solve quadratic equations by factoring, by completing the square, or by applying a theorem for solving radical equations, and not have any idea of how these methods fit together—or even that they *do* fit together.

Similarly, you can learn parts of a subject with no idea of how those parts fit into *the whole.* That also happens with algebra. Very few students finish a course in algebra with an idea of what the whole of algebra is. Many students' experience with a history course is learning lists of events, dates, people, and the relations among them, but with very little idea of what the history of that time and place was *as a whole.*

If you have had that experience, what you were missing was *the logic of* that subject matter. Understanding a whole is not the same as understanding the parts. It is not even the same as understanding *all* of the parts. Instead, it is understanding parts as they fit together with one another logically, and understanding them as they form a coherent whole: a logic.

Thinking critically in a field is getting hold of the logic of that field. The concept of "the logic of" something is one of the most important concepts in learning to think critically.

Take the U.S. Constitution. You can memorize the entire Constitution (Preamble, 7 articles, 26 amendments) and still not *know* the Constitution in any real sense. Professors of constitutional law probably never memorize it at all. They know the Constitution in quite a different sense. They understand, for example, how to extrapolate from constitutional principles to situations that did not exist at the time the Constitution was written. They understand alternative ways it can be reasonably applied in an era of nuclear secrets, universal adult voting, *Miranda* rights, and the abolition of separate but equal schooling. They understand *the logic of* the Constitution. To call it "the" logic does not mean that there is only one such logic—there are several in fact. But it means that there are coherent ways of thinking through and in terms of the Constitution. It means that the Constitution has a distinct set of purposes, which fit together with the assumptions, implications, alternative readings, interpretations, central concepts, key questions at issue, and distinctive points of view embodied in it. (These elements of reasoning are the subject of Chapter 3.) Understanding the Constitution is understanding the logic sufficiently to be able to reason within it.

You can also approach the concept of "the logic of" by considering what you do when you forget something you have learned in a field. Suppose you have memorized something in a course—the dates of the Civil War, for example, or Hobbes' second law of nature, or whether a U- or a V-shaped valley is the result of glaciation. And then you forget it. Because you learned it by memory, you have no recourse but to look it up and then memorize it again. But people who know the logic of a subject won't have to look it up if they happen to forget a detail. Instead, they can *figure it out*. ("Figuring it out" is almost a synonym for "critical thinking.") They can figure it out from the events that they know led up to the Civil War and the other events they know followed from it, or from understanding Hobbes' idea of a state of nature and the social contract. They can figure out the shape of a glaciated valley by envisioning how glaciers move, and drawing conclusions.

Some things, however, do not have a logic to them. In that case, all you can do is memorize the individual bits of information. You can't figure such things out, because there is no rhyme or reason to them. Peoples' first names are like that. You can't look at someone intently and then figure out that her first name is Janis. In cities and towns, street names may or may not have a logic. If Oak Street is followed by Main, that gives no clue as to what the next street is. There is no logic to it. Sometimes, however, there *is* a logic: if 24th Street is followed by 25th, it doesn't take much effort to figure out what the next street is likely to be. In that situation, street names have a logic.

The subjects taught in school, however, are almost never composed of unrelated individual bits of information. If it seems that way to you, that's only because you have missed the logic of that subject. (There are a few exceptions to this rule; e. g., the keyboard skills used in typing have no logic.[6] But such exceptions are rare. And it is no coincidence that there is no *field* of typing.)

What Does the Logic of a Field Consist Of?

Ultimately, we can display the logic of a field by analyzing it in terms of the *elements of reasoning*. The elements are the most central concepts of critical thinking and form the substance of Chapter 3. An abbreviated example of a student's analysis follows in the box below.

As you read it, notice how Jerel has a grasp of the field as a whole. He analyzes the field—breaks it down into its essential parts— but he also synthesizes it. This is, of course, not *all* there is to physics. And it is not the only version of a logic of physics. But it assembles fundamental parts of physics for us, displays a vision of the whole of it, and shows how the parts are interrelated.

The value of an analysis like this does not consist so much in reading it as in creating it, in thinking it out. Once you have constructed it, your understanding of details will fit into this logic in a coherent way, and as your understanding deepens, the logic will grow deeper as well.

This is a way of getting at the logic of a field, but there are other ways as well: learning the vocabulary of the field, grasping the fundamental and powerful concepts of a field, and thinking in terms of the central questions of a field.

There are several <u>purposes</u> of physics, and one of the most important is to understand the fundamental laws that govern the interaction of matter and energy.

Some of the <u>assumptions</u> of physics are that rigorous scientific explanations of natural phenomena are superior to other explanations offered by non-scientific areas. The world physics studies is the actual world and not a fictitious creation, and it exists independent of humans. Complex systems can be analyzed and understood in terms of simpler systems, and therefore ultimately all phenomena can be explained by physics. Physics uses mathematics as its language and assumes physical systems can have math applied to them and that the axioms of math are correct. . . .

Some of the <u>implications and consequences</u> of physics are that understanding natural phenomena is not restricted to the gifted few, but to all humans; and that every human can act on the world by using the concepts of physics. Useful technologies can be constructed by using natural phenomena.

The <u>information</u>, <u>data</u> and <u>evidence</u> that physics uses come from all physical actions and interactions. For example, planetary motion, electron tunneling, refraction, etc. It uses this data to create general predictive models and consistent theories. These theories, as long as they continue to work, provide evidence for physics by predicting and explaining various phenomena. The theories also provide information about how energy and matter behave in certain situations.

Some of the <u>concepts</u> of physics include the existence and conservation of energy, matter, momentum, and charge; the use of fields to describe forces at a distance, and the concepts underlying quantum mechanics and relativity.

The <u>conclusions</u> physics draws: experiments are about the behavior of matter such as the nature of light, the speed of light as the maximum speed of a signal, heat as a measure of energy. In its natural state an object has no acceleration. Magnetic poles exist only in pairs.

Some of the <u>questions</u> physics is trying to answer are: What is the ultimate building block of matter? What kinds of cosmological objects exist? What is the nature and fate of the universe, and how did it begin? Can all the elementary forces of nature be united and explained by one theory? Physics is also interested in answering more practical problems such as how to get cleaner and more efficient energy sources, and how to use energy most efficiently.

From the <u>point of view</u> of physics, it is the basic experimental science that all other sciences must reduce to because it studies the most basic elementary processes, objects, and interactions. . . .

Like other natural sciences, physics exists in a <u>context</u> of scientific method and rigorous testing of theories. In its <u>historical context,</u> physics developed from the ancient Greeks, particularly Aristotle, but modern physics and scientific method begin with the "natural philosophy" of Galileo and Newton.

There are <u>alternative</u> emphases in physics. Some of the main ones are classical mechanics, quantum mechanics, relativity theory; theoretical versus experimental physics; physics and its relation to technology and engineering.

(The underlined terms in each entry are the *elements*.)

Learning the Vocabulary of the Discipline

How can you begin to think in terms of the logic of the discipline you're studying? A good place to start is learning and using the discipline's vocabulary. This is a minimal condition, and it is easy to confuse means and ends. Learning the vocabulary in a field is *a means* to an end. It is an essential means for learning to reason better in the field. But you have to be careful not to think that learning the vocabulary—learning the *names* for concepts in the field—is somehow the *point* of studying in the field. It isn't. Teachers don't stress learning terminology because it's the purpose of the course. Rather, it's that the purpose cannot be accomplished without the terminology. Learning the parts of a flower in a botany course is important, but it is seldom an end in itself. (It is for some people. Some people find value in knowing the precise names of things.) For most people, the vocabulary is important because it increases their ability to think clearly about flowers, to communicate clearly about botany, to gain precision in their observations. These abilities in turn provide insight beyond flowers, insight into how things grow, into fundamental processes of life.

What Is It to Think in a Discipline's Vocabulary?

Of course, it's not the same as merely memorizing definitions. Haven't you often memorized definitions of terms without really having a handle on what they mean, without being able to use them intelligibly?

Disciplines are integrated wholes and their vocabulary reflects that. Vocabulary in a discipline is like a web: it's interconnected. Thinking of one vocabulary word brings up its connections to other words in the vocabulary. It starts you thinking in terms of logical connections, rather than in terms of fragments. It also brings up the connections between the concepts that lie behind the words. For example, the term *force* in physics should lead you naturally, almost automatically, to think about *mass* and *acceleration*. In an English literature course, the term *stream of consciousness* should bring James Joyce's *Ulysses* to your mind, at least as a background, ready to be applied. In social work, when you think about "enabling behavior," your mind turns naturally to dysfunctionality, control, needs, and a web of other terms.

There is another advantage to learning the vocabulary of the field. Your present vocabulary is saturated with the point of view you grew up with. It has its own connections, and often these run counter to the more accurate, precise, and important connections that have been discovered in the discipline. So, if you think in your present vocabulary of something *in motion*, you are liable to connect to the idea of "something else that puts it in motion" (a *force*). That's natural, but it is the direct opposite of what we learn from Newton. In Newtonian theory (and in reality) "being in motion" connects to the idea that *nothing* is moving it (*no* net forces); in reality, things that are moving simply keep moving. (Only when they turn or move *faster* is there a connection to the idea that there is a force moving them.)

The concept of *enabling* in social work is a dramatic example. We often think of helping people who are in a recurring state of need (e.g., helping an alcoholic make it home) as a *good* act, as an act of mercy or unselfishness. Thinking in terms of *enabling*, though, shifts these connections and calls them into question. Now, connections are made to how the one who seems to be helping may be perpetuating a *dysfunctionality* in the person, and how the *enabler* may be *controlling* the situation to meet his or her own *needs*.

To change your way of thinking, you need to change the vocabulary of your thinking.

Fundamental and Powerful Concepts

Here are two basic questions about learning a discipline:

1. If I take a course in a discipline, how can I think critically *within* that discipline?
2. How do I learn to think critically while *also* amassing the large amount of information—often misleadingly called the content—I may need to learn in the course?

When confronted with these questions, students, and sometimes teachers, often phrase them in terms of a false opposition. They think they have to choose *either* to learn critical thinking *or* to learn content—as if the two were opposed.

They are not at all opposed. Learning content *is* learning to think. If I learn content, but I don't learn to think in terms of that content, then it's not *content* at all. It's just *words*, memorized and soon forgotten words. If I learn that for every action there is an equal and opposite reaction, but can't explain what that phrase means when given the example of a man pushing a *stationary* wall (what is the *reaction*?), then all I have is a sing-song slogan. That is not *content*. Content is not repeating formulas or slogans, nor is it memorizing long lists of information. Rather, I have ownership of a course's content when I *understand* the course concepts, see their implications, relate them to other concepts; when I can raise relevant questions about them, when I can apply them to new situations.

The answer to both questions 1 and 2 has to do with fundamental and powerful concepts.

Understanding Fundamental and Powerful (f&p) Concepts

What are fundamental and powerful concepts? A **fundamental and powerful concept** is one that can be used to explain or think out a huge body of questions, problems, information, and situations. All fields have f&p concepts, but there are a relatively small number of them in any particular area. They are *the* most central and useful ideas in the discipline. They are to be contrasted with individual bits of information, or with less general concepts. In the earlier example, "cell" is a far more fundamental and powerful concept than "mitochondria." The idea, then, is that if you can understand the f&p concepts in a deep way, you are in a position to understand a great deal of the rest of the course. You need to learn to *think in terms of* the fundamental and powerful concepts, to use them to think through any new problem or question that arises.

For example, when I was in college, I liked poetry, particularly the Romantic poets: Keats, Shelley, Wordsworth, and so forth. So I took a course in the Romantics. Here is all that I remember from the course: *Michael*, 1800. That is, I remember that Wordsworth's poem, *Michael*, was written in 1800. That is the sole remnant left from more than 200 names of poems and dates that I memorized in that course. This is an example of the opposite of an f&p concept. It is a detail, and it illuminates nothing beyond itself. What would be an f&p concept in that course? Well, one would clearly be the concept of *romanticism* itself. Romanticism involves a whole way of looking at life: a feeling of deep yearning, a longing for the unknown, the richness of imagination, an intense love of nature, especially for the mystery of nature, for the faraway and the unattainable.

What makes romanticism a fundamental and powerful concept is that once you grasp it deeply, you acquire a concept for understanding and appreciating many Romantic poems. You can then take almost any poem written during that period, understand it as an expression of romanticism, and think it through using the concept of romanticism. That gives you an insight into those poems that you would not have without that concept. Additionally, if you have questions about how those poets lived; their attitudes toward politics, love, drugs, or religion; or about novels and essays written at the time—you can now think through any of these questions using the concept of romanticism. It is a *powerful* concept.

But the case is far stronger than this: if you can learn to think in terms of f&p concepts—in this case, *romanticism*—then not only are many questions in the course illuminated, but also any number of questions *beyond* the course, ones that arise long after the course is over. How does romanticism apply to later poets you may read? How does it apply to your own poetry? How about movies? The topics can go on and on. Romanticism is powerful as a concept because it continues to illuminate, far beyond the subject matter of the course. How do you look at *your life* in terms of romanticism? How about the romanticism of science, or the law? What are the romantic aspects of your choice of profession, your choices in romantic relationships (the other sense of "romantic"), your self-image? How does it help you understand yourself and others?

The concept is *fundamental* because it forms the foundation of our understanding of that era, and of a great many forms of life that extend beyond that era. It is *powerful* because it is useful in understanding a wide range of questions and problems, issues and situations.

Although romanticism is a concept that is important in *understanding* certain phenomena, fundamental and powerful concepts are just as important in fields that emphasize *doing.*

Take the nursing concept *asepsis.* There are many antiseptic procedures, both medical and surgical, some suitable in one situation, some in another, and each of them has a subset of steps associated with it. It is very important to learn these. The trouble is that, as a student nurse, you can spend so much time learning these individual procedures that you lose the forest for the trees. It's easy to become engaged in parroting and carrying out rote procedures, rather than assessing what to do in a situation by thinking it out. Every nursing teacher has scary stories of things like this occurring. So the idea is: take any situation that arises and think it out with the idea of *asepsis* in mind. How can this situation be kept *aseptic?* With that in mind, you can identify the specific antiseptic procedures called for by a specific situation. If you have to adapt the procedure to an unusual situation, you have a way of doing so—namely, thinking in terms of how to achieve *asepsis.* It is not a surefire way, of course. There *are no* surefire ways. But it is a good way, a reasonable way. If, on the other hand, all you have done is *memorize* the specific procedures, you can't determine which part you've forgotten, and you have no insight into why a particular procedure is appropriate for an unusual case. In fact, you may have no real grasp of what a procedure is *for:* it may be just a procedure you follow blindly. When new procedures come along, long after graduation, you have no broader concepts through which to understand them.

To think critically through the course, these f&p concepts need to be learned in a *deep* way. Almost certainly, the teacher of the course I took in Romantic poetry did define romanticism. But it remained just that—a definition. For me, the student, it was one more detail, on a par with "*Michael,* 1800." By contrast, fundamental and powerful concepts should constantly return throughout the course as part of the explanatory context whenever new material is introduced. Given *any* new material, the question you should always raise is: How is this illuminated by our small stock of f&p concepts? Occasionally, it may be that some new material is not illuminated at all by one of the f&p concepts. That's okay. You should recognize that too. Maybe you should ask about it in class. But what you are aiming for is to make those f&p concepts part of *the way you think.*

All courses have f&p concepts: *homeostasis* in biology is an example, the concept of *the audience* is one that is central to all writing courses, the concept of *what is justifiable* is at the heart of any ethics course. Most courses and fields have more than one, but not a large number. If you start thinking in terms of 10 or 15 concepts, or more, you are already going beyond the fundamental ones to narrower, more specific concepts. Focus instead on a smaller number, trying to get at what is most central. The important things are

- to identify the f&p concepts,
- to understand how they fit together,
- to learn them in a deep way,
- to use them in your thinking about every important question or problem that arises in the course,
- to use them to begin to think through questions that lie beyond the scope of the course.

IDENTIFYING F&P CONCEPTS

Depending on how far along you are in your course, you may not yet be able to identify the fundamental and powerful concepts. Your teacher may have told you the most f&p concepts. If so, do not treat that as just another piece of information. Rather, take those concepts and use them to think out every single important topic or question that arises in the course.

If you are far enough along:

1. Focus on the course as a whole, not on individual parts.

2. Identify three f&p concepts that underlie the whole course. Do this by first identifying *one*. Only then, go on to identify two others that stem from that one. (Use the concept map in Figure 2.1.)

3. Share and discuss the f&p concepts with other students. How do they underlie the field or course as a whole? Are they fundamental enough? The concepts each class member identifies should be similar.

FIGURE 2.1 *A concept map.*

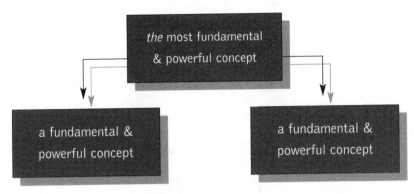

Using Concept Maps to Display Logical Connections

Concept maps are a useful way of showing the logical connections that exist between concepts. For example, the field of clinical psychology trains therapists to deal with the psychological disorders of patients. When clinical psychologists work they focus on diagnosing the patient, on identifying the major causes of the psychological disorder in that patient, and carrying out a course of treatment. We can identify five main concepts, then: *clinical psychology, psychological disorders, diagnosis, causes,* and *treatment.*

A concept map of these might be drawn as in Figure 2.2.

FIGURE 2.2 *A concept map for psychological disorders.*

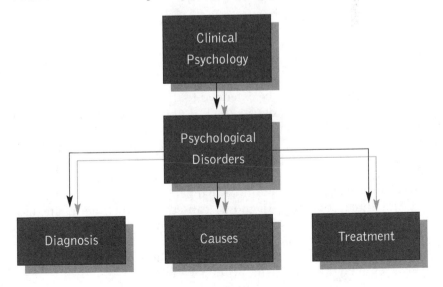

That's not the only way to map out these concepts, however. You may reason instead that the treatment a clinical psychologist recommends for a patient is not *separate* from the diagnosis and causes, as it is portrayed in Figure 2.2. Treatment *depends* on the diagnosis the psychologist gives and on the causes of the disorder in that patient. Such reasoning might be depicted as in the map in Figure 2.3.

FIGURE 2.3 *An alternative concept map for psychological disorders.*

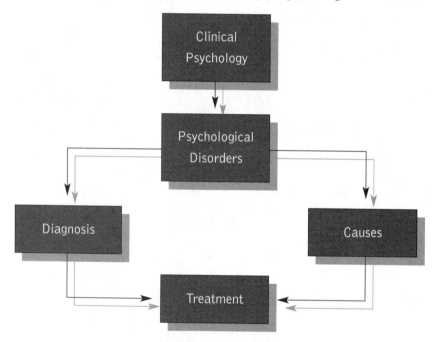

The concept map reflects the system of thinking, the logical connections between concepts.

The concept map can be extended to display new problems in the field. Thus, an important debate in clinical psychology centers around psychotherapy versus drug therapy. Many psychologists contend that drug therapy treats only symptoms, not the condition itself, and that powerful medications often have serious side effects. The primary concepts of this debate can be identified as: *psychotherapy, drug therapy, symptoms, side effects.*[7] They can be mapped as shown in Figure 2.4.

The three concepts, diagnosis, causes, and treatment, are f&p concepts in clinical psychology. That means that, as you learn to think the way a clinical psychologist thinks, you can reason out virtually any question in the field in terms of how to diagnose it, what its causes are, and how it should best be treated.

FIGURE 2.4 *An extension of the concept map for psychological disorders.*

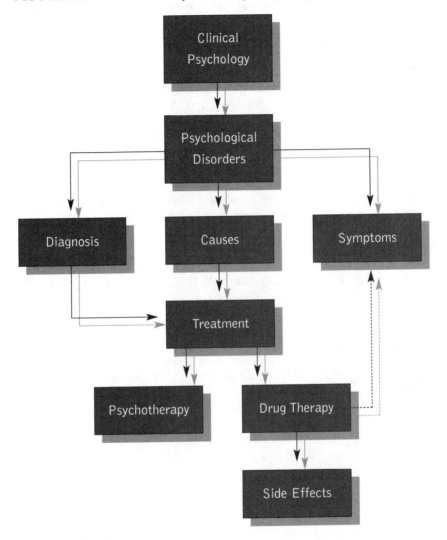

The Central Question of the Course as a Whole

There is one other important way to keep your thinking in the course on track, to grasp the logic of the field. It is to think in terms of *the central question* of the course as a whole.

A course in a field has a central question that it revolves around. It is the unifying question, and everything in the course fits into that question. The way to understand every item in the course, to see how it all fits together, is to understand it in terms of that central question. Take this book. The central question it addresses is: *How can you learn to think critically in a field or discipline?* Every topic discussed in the book is an aspect of that central question. So, if you have difficulty understanding how implications fit with assumptions, or if you wonder, *How do the impediments discussed in Chapter 1 fit with the standards in Chapter 4?*, the way to think it out is to ask, *How do these fit together to help me learn to think critically in the field?* That central question forms the unifying center around which all other topics and questions are organized. Without keeping that central question in mind, the parts of a book (or a course) fall apart into separate and unrelated pieces.

One problem with describing a central question is that it can seem so simple. And it *is* simple—simple in the sense of uncomplicated, not in the sense of easy. Insights that are simple in that sense are often the things that are most worth saying.

Picture yourself taking a course in educational psychology. You are deluged with educational theories, countertheories, procedures, statistics, case studies, definitions, objectives, and a hundred other items. All of them seem important. This one relates to that one, this other one doesn't. This theorist says X, this other theorist says Y, and a third says Z. In such cases, it sometimes seems almost heroic to see the forest for the trees.

What is the central question? It is, *How does a student learn? And how can I help students learn?*[8] That is what educational psychology is all about. *Everything* in the course is geared to that one question. You are taking this course in education to get a richer, fuller understanding of how students learn, and how you as teacher can help them learn. To think through any issue critically during the course means to think it through *in terms of* how it contributes to answering that central question. That question provides the structure through which everything else is understood.

There can be more than one central question in a course. It is usually helpful to assume that there is only one because it unifies your vision of the course and the field. But you may have to suspend that assumption. For example, the central question in a literature course might be: *How can literature enrich and deepen the way I live my life?* That is a profound and far-reaching question. The whole course, every assignment, every poem, drama, or story, and all class discussion, can be seen as addressing that single, central question. But that same course might have another central question. It might focus on the *craft* of writing: *What do writers do to make literature effective?* That is also a central question, one that directs your attention to how writers accomplish what they accomplish: how they use characters, theme, plot, conflict, and literary forms. A third central question might focus on the interaction necessary to make meaning: *How do writer, reader, and society together create meaning in literature?* This too is a question that may underlie the entire course. It directs you to ask, whenever you read *any* piece of literature, in the course or long afterward, *How do we, together, make this work of art?*

Thinking in terms of central questions can change your whole understanding of a course. A good candidate for an f&p concept in physical education, for example, is *lifelong fitness.* A central question could be: *How can I promote lifelong fitness?* That is, the suggestion is to think of every activity in a physical education course in relation to how it promotes, or detracts from, lifelong fitness. You can now think through nutrition, sports, and exercise in a different, more global way. Notice how thinking in terms of that central question—and *lifelong fitness*—can change your perception of potentially damaging sports like football or boxing, at least as part of a physical education program.

Thinking in terms of the central question may seem easy, but it's actually difficult. It takes practice and focused attention. It doesn't come naturally. Think about other classes you have taken, and notice how many of them you sat through, from beginning to end, without ever asking yourself the central questions underlying the class, without ever understanding that there *was* one.

A central question is difficult the way a mission statement is difficult. A business, university, hospital, or organization may formulate a mission statement. Many individuals also formulate a personal mission statement. It is a way to keep themselves focused on what is important, and allow what's less important to drift away. A person's mission might be "My mission is to respect myself, others, and all things." It is often difficult to formulate a mission statement that captures what you truly think is important, what you think your mission is. By the same token, though, formulating it can be deeply enlightening.

What's even more difficult, however, is keeping the mission in front of you as you go through life: remembering it, keeping it fresh, not letting it become an empty formula, reviewing it as you mature, actually living your life, as much as possible, in accord with it.

The central question of a course operates the same way, and it is dif-

Identify, as well as you can at the beginning of the semester, the central question of the course as a whole.

Then, respond to the central question briefly, in a paragraph or two.

Respond to the question again near the middle of the semester, and a third time near the end.

Compare how the responses you've given have changed and deepened.

Some examples of central questions for a few courses:

- Chemistry: How are you and the world around you created by chemicals?

- Composition: What *is it* to write an effective essay?

- Economics: How is society shaped by the decisions people make on the basis of expected costs and benefits?

- Philosophy: How can you make sense of your life and of the world around you?

The important thing about a central question, however, is not merely to *ask* it. It is to *use it in your thinking* at every point in the course.

ficult in the same way. Like a mission statement, it is a question you can ask yourself over and over. As your education and understanding increase, the depth with which you answer that question will also increase.

- Formulate the central question(s) of the course as a whole.
- Break it down into two or three subsidiary questions. Then figure out how they fit together within the central question.
- Look at every topic in the course and ask: *How does it fit into the central question? How does that topic contribute to answering the central question?*
- Remind yourself of the central question frequently, especially at times when you feel overwhelmed or when you find yourself just going through the motions.
- Reformulate the central question from time to time.
- Push the envelope. Ask, *How is that central question important for your life beyond the classroom?*

Impediments to Critical Thinking Within a Discipline

The impediments to critical thinking mentioned in Chapter 1 are impediments to thinking critically within a discipline as well. For example, two of the impediments deal with forming a picture of the world based on what we learn from news reports or on what we see in movies, TV, advertising, and other fictionalized accounts. But these sources can also provide us with an uncritical picture of the subject matter in courses that we study.

For example, space travel is presented matter-of-factly in fictionalized accounts (often at "warp speed," with stars streaking by, and the "noise" of booster rockets firing). We also see news reports of spacecraft sending incredibly precise data back from Mars or Jupiter. We also hear reputable scientists talk about black holes and the consequent possibility of wormholes through space-time. These are three separate sources of information that really have almost nothing to do with one another: fiction, news bites, scientific reports. But many people put them together uncritically and assume that space travel to other planetary systems is just around the corner. They form an unrealistic picture, one that can easily be an impediment to learning about science. Space travel beyond our tiny system of planets is unlikely ever to happen. Distances are simply too great, our highest speeds are infinitesimally small, and there are physical limits (not just practical limits) to what objects with mass can do. Human space travel beyond the solar system cannot be proved impossible, of course, but it's only a fantasy, probably no more likely than finding out that there actually are leprechauns.

You can readily find examples of how the other impediments discussed in Chapter 1 can seriously interfere with your ability to think critically through the subject matter in your courses. Think of the *fear* so many people have about taking math or science and how this interferes with reasoning through questions that are entirely within their capacity; or the way we *stereotype* social scientists, nurses, professors, CEOs, psychiatrists; or the way even within a discipline people *egocentrically* identify with one position or another and go to unreasonable extremes to defend that position; or, *developmentally*, the way a need to feel safe can lead people to major in a subject where they feel in control, even though their real interest is in a different subject entirely.

Background Stories, Background Logic

There are other impediments to critical thinking in a discipline. We enter courses not as blank slates, but with *background stories* and accounts already in place. These stories have a logic that shapes how we think within the discipline. We have a story, for example, about chemicals: chemistry teachers sometimes despair at the persistent background story that if something is made of chemicals, it is therefore bad for you. Chemistry teachers respond to this background story by teaching that this can't be true because *everything* is made of chemicals. As a student though, you can hear what your chemistry teacher says, you can write it in your notes, you can give the right answer on exams—and even after all that, once class is over, you can still believe that chemicals are bad for you. It is extremely difficult, for example, to understand what it means when biochemists say that *life* is chemistry.

Though these examples are from science, background stories are strong impediments to critical thinking in all fields. You have in you right now, like a default program on your computer, background stories about how business works (including marketing, management, accounting, . . .), what nursing and education are (including all the specializations), how humans interact (psychology, sociology, political science, . . .), what other cultures are like (anthropology, history, . . .), what reality is like (philosophy, science, religious studies, . . .), how to find answers (librarianship, methods courses, math, . . .). It is not so much that these background stories you have are *false.* Many of them *are* false, but even if the story has a lot of truth in it, it is probably a very limited truth, and the story will be deeply misleading when it is extended beyond the area where it works.

Even calling them "stories" is misleading because that implies that the stories are easily supplanted with new information from your courses. But that doesn't do justice to how deep our background stories run and to how pervasive their influence is. It is hard for the account you learn in your course to get through. Background stories are deep and pervasive in part because they are unexamined, and in part because they have *a logic* to them. That is, our background stories are not just stories; rather, they embody a whole way of thinking about things.

Here is another example. Most people have a picture of how evolution is supposed to work according to Darwinism. Yet, that picture is deeply misguided, often straight-out wrong. How many of the following do you think of as part of the theory of evolution?

- Life progresses by evolution.
- There are higher and lower forms of life.
- Evolution has something to do with how individuals adapt to their environment.
- The fittest organisms tend to survive.
- Organisms have a drive (or an instinct) to reproduce.
- Organisms also have a drive (or an instinct) for self-preservation.
- Evolution has something to do with whether an individual survives.
- Humans are more evolutionarily advanced than chimps.
- The better an organism is able to adapt to its environment, the more likely it is to evolve.

Try to picture this as a real situation rather than just an exercise in a book: Suppose you are on a wooden stepladder about 6 feet off the ground, and the step you are standing on breaks unexpectedly; and suppose that there are three bars next to you that you might catch to stop your fall, one at eye-level, another at waist-level, and a third at knee-level. Which bar will you be able to grab?

See footnote #9 for an answer.

Think about farming in the Soviet Union under communism. Farms in the USSR were owned collectively (i.e., by "the state"); the people who worked the farms did not own them. Even if you know only very little about the subject, you probably know the answer to this question: Why doesn't collective farming work?

Formulate an answer before you go on.

See footnote #10 for an answer.

- We live today in the age of mammals; there was once an age of dinosaurs.
- Humans evolved from monkeys or apes.
- Humans are more fit to survive than dinosaurs.
- Humans are advancing evolutionarily in their intelligence.

Notice how these statements have a logic to them: we can reason from one idea to another. We can reason from progress *to* higher forms of life, *to* advanced ability to adapt, *to* greater survival, *to* humans as the high point of evolution.

But *all* the statements are deeply flawed. A few of them can be made to fit in with evolution, but only by wrenching them from their ordinary meaning. This whole way of reasoning seriously distorts everything that the theory of evolution is about. Yet, if you are convinced of any of the statements that make up this logic, you probably cannot get hold of how in the world it could be wrong.

Background stories are so difficult to counteract because they are virtually invisible. We don't see them as background stories at all. We see them simply as *the way things are*. As a result, the background stories influence our interpretation of everything we encounter. We don't even *hear* that the account we learn in our courses contradicts our background story.

So, as a student you need to be on the lookout for how your background stories influence the way you interpret the subject matter. You need to realize when they lead you to dismiss the topics in your course as unimportant to your life. You need to notice when contradictions arise between the subject-matter account in the classroom and your "common-sense" account. When you identify a contradiction, take it seriously, and use it to challenge the background story you hold without being aware of it.

Simply becoming aware of our background stories is empowering because it means we can decide what we are going to believe, and, if we choose, we can decide that by reasoning things out.

School Stuff

Another impediment to critical thinking in a discipline can be illustrated by a couple of math problems Kurt Reusser asked fourth graders.[11]

There are 26 sheep and 10 goats on a ship. How old is the captain?

Most children *add* 26 and 10 to find the age of the captain! Not only that, but the better they are at math, the more likely they are to add to find the age of the captain.

Here is a second problem asked of the fourth graders:

A school is going on a field trip, and they need school buses. There are 140 kids in the school, and each school bus holds 30 kids. How many school buses do they need in all?

The children's answer is "Four, remainder 20"!

What is going on with these answers? It is not that the children cannot do the math. It's that, for the children, there is simply no link between math and reality. For them, math is something you learn in school, and it has nothing to do with real captains or real school buses.

Most of us have this category called *school stuff*. It is the stuff we hear about in school, and we keep all this stuff in a special receptacle in our minds. We think, "I have to jump through some hoops to become a nurse, and one of them is taking courses in basic science. But there is no need for me to remember that stuff. It's *just science;* it's *not nursing.*"

Our tendency to classify the material in the discipline as school stuff is hard to combat. Teachers have all had the experience of talking about something interesting, but as soon as students realize that it won't be on the test, many of them just tune out: the stuff is important only for taking tests.

The way to learn to think critically, in your life and in your courses, is to think in terms of the logic of the discipline, to apply what you learn to your life, and to look for those links particularly if the material in the discipline is hard to understand. One ironic aspect of thinking in terms of "school stuff" is that by taking the material seriously, organizing it, and applying it to your own life, you will actually do better on exams than you will by cramming school stuff.

The temptation to isolate course material as merely school stuff is heightened by ingrained study techniques: passive listening, memorizing information rather than organizing and synthesizing it, simply repeating information from the book or a lecture, not formulating questions. If I think of what I learn in my courses primarily as stuff to be put into notes and regurgitated on exams, there is little chance I will learn much. I will leave class with the same unexamined background stories. These are difficult patterns to break, and it's difficult to make the leap of faith that using critical thinking as a study tool will actually result in better school performance.

Even being good at talking or good at writing can impede critical thinking. There are people, for example, who are particularly good at thinking quickly on their feet and presenting their views orally or in writing. They always seem to have a ready answer and a way to defend it. Teachers often praise them for their quickness or intelligence. They may be skilled at deflecting the tough questions. They may be able to write vividly and persuasively. If I am that kind of person, this type of talent can set up a background logic in which I start to think of school as a place to showcase my abilities, but where there is no need to take the subject seriously. The talent can actually close off paths I could take to enrich my life; it can make me comfortable with limiting my choices. But when used in the service of effective thinking, such talents can increase the value of learning the discipline.

It is important to take the subject matter as *your own,* to participate in the construction of your own knowledge.

With that in mind, review some of your personal history. Think back on courses you took more than two years ago:

- What is an example of something you learned in a course that still has major importance in your thinking or in your life?

- What is an example of a course you took that had *no* long-term influence on your life?

Now ask yourself, "How can I make this present course I am taking more like the first example? How can I use it to bring *value* to my life?"

Trusting the Discipline

Talking about trusting the discipline, in the context of critical thinking, implies two seemingly contradictory messages: first, that critical thinking encourages you to question the discipline you are studying; but, second, that it's reasonable for you to trust the discipline you are studying. Each message is reasonable, and each can be exaggerated.

Questioning lies at the heart of critical thinking, and a student in a discipline will be questioning many aspects of it: how to analyze the course material, how to apply it to cases, how to compare and contrast different theories, how to organize the main concepts, and how to evaluate positions in the discipline itself. In a political science course, for example, you may be asked to compare and contrast various political systems, to evaluate them, and maybe to reject one or another. In an ethics course, you may be asked to evaluate competing arguments about the morality of abortion or killing animals for food, and maybe come to a well-reasoned decision.

That questioning attitude can leave you with the impression that a goal of critical thinking is to be skeptical about what you learn in a discipline. This is particularly true when the course covers topics that you've experienced firsthand—relationships, sports, dieting, family, power structures, art. It's easy to feel that the course material is simply talk. You can leave the course with your ideas about those topics completely unaffected. Or, having read competing accounts of marriage, you can come to believe that everyone in the field has his or her own theory about the subject. You can conclude that each account of marriage is just one of many, with no better backing than a host of others. It can become something to be doubted automatically, certainly no better than your own view of marriage, or the one you were brought up with.

The idea that the subject matter is just "school stuff" can increase that skepticism. At the least, it can lead you to the impression that course content is not something to be taken too seriously. You can quickly say, "There are so many different views about political systems or abortion or marriage, that I am no better off than when I entered the course. It's all just a matter of opinion." But that would be a mistake.

To a great degree, the findings in a discipline, the material presented in texts and courses in that discipline, can be trusted. When you think about it, compared to other sources of knowledge in our society, the content of the disciplines studied in school can be trusted to a remarkable degree.

Disciplines do have built-in sources of distortion, and you need to be aware of these. For example, experts in the discipline are much more trustworthy in their central results than they are in their application of those results to actual situations, especially complex situations. Thus, in physics we know the laws that govern physical processes such as the weather, but that doesn't mean physics can tell us what the temperature will be a week from Thursday in Colorado Springs. It can't. (As paradoxical as it sounds, it seems that physics can be used to prove that we will never be able to predict next week's exact weather on the basis of physics.) Another source of distortion is that discipline experts are as human as anyone, so they can be guided by egocentricity and developmental factors just the way you and I can. A third source of distortion is actually rooted in a *strength* of the discipline: disciplines by their nature cannot pay attention to all factors that affect a situation. A discipline pays attention only to those factors that it studies. Thus, if you are studying adolescent development in a psychology class, you are learning to think the way a developmental psychologist thinks. You get insight into adolescents by looking at their patterns of physical, cognitive, social, and personality changes, based primarily on experiments and correlational studies. In thinking the way a psychologist thinks, you concentrate on the psychological factors in adolescent development, and not on the anthropological, legal, economic, medical, and literary factors.

It is important, then, not to accept the discipline without question. As a student, though, it is hard to appreciate how much emphasis is usually placed on critical thinking standards by teachers in their presentations, by the authors of textbooks, by scholars in the field. Very seldom is a book used in a course "just someone's opinion." Editorials in newspapers, on the other hand, are completely different. Some columnists are very careful, try to avoid distortion, and attempt to report both sides of an issue fairly. But most function much the way advertisers do: they try to influence you to accept their own view of the matter. In contrast, virtually any textbook on controversial issues presents many different viewpoints. Authors of texts work hard to eliminate bias. (A frequent criticism of textbooks is that they *include too many* points of view rather than too few, that they are *bland* rather than biased.) Scholarly work is scrutinized by others in the field (peer review) who have extensive knowledge and skills. (One observation is that in science [in contrast to dogmatic areas] no one is praised more than someone who *refutes* accepted theories.) None of this implies that authors are always successful in eliminating bias or egocentricity. Of course not. But they are far more successful than people who don't even try to root out bias, or who present only their own side of an issue.

Trusting a discipline, then, does not mean believing it completely or automatically. It means taking it seriously, treating it as something to be learned from, rather than as something to be doubted automatically or put aside or rejected out of hand. After consideration, you may reject an idea or find it inadequate in one

Suppose you are presented with a theoretical analysis of the family in a sociology course.[12] A structural-functional analysis analyzes the family as having four basic functions: (1) it socializes people, teaching both children and adults how to integrate into society; (2) it regulates sexual activity; (3) it confers social identity (race, religion, class, etc.); and (4) it provides material and emotional security.

You are engaged in critical thinking, so you clearly need to analyze this model. You need to ask questions about the elements of reasoning (Chapter 3), such as:

What is the purpose of the model?

What assumptions are being made in it?

What are the implications of accepting this model?

What reputable alternative models of the family are there?

You will also need to evaluate the model according to standards of critical thinking (Chapter 4), such as:

How accurate is the model?

How adequate is it? Are there aspects of the family that it does not account for?

How deep does it go? Is it broad enough to cover the diversity of families in the world?

But what you should not do is dismiss this structural-functional analysis as just school stuff. It is not critical thinking to be simply skeptical about it: "I don't know. It doesn't ring true to me." It is not critical thinking to raise questions simply to avoid having to take something seriously: "I read that 'Analysis of the Family' section. But what I wonder is how accurate, clear, and adequate it is. So I don't buy it." Those are good questions to raise, but they are questions that *begin* the inquiry, not ones that shut it down.

There are not many different theoretical analyses of the family, nor is there a different one for every writer in the field. Sociology texts offer only four. Each of the four offers something powerful and illuminating. Each has far more explanatory weight than any unexamined common-sense view of the family.

way or another. But to trust a discipline means to "try it on," to think in terms of it and see how it helps you understand the world in a new and richer way.

It is reasonable to apply a similar degree of trust even in matters that are far more controversial and deeply personal. For many people, for example, understanding the Bible is a deeply personal and intensely significant part of their lives. But, if you want to find out what the Bible is saying, if that is important to you, a reasonable way to go about it is to take a course in Biblical studies. The authors you are likely to read in such a course will be Biblical scholars, familiar with a wide variety of viewpoints and interpretations—not just with others who agree with them. They have read primary sources carefully. They have come to reasoned conclusions about the dating of manuscripts, and when and by whom those manuscripts were written. Most likely they know the original languages. They are intimately familiar with both the historical periods and the archaeological record. Their writings have been subjected to peer review.

Such extensive research is not found in most other sources you might consult, such as television documentaries, sermons you may hear by religious leaders, evangelists on the radio, or the newest *New York Times* best-seller.

Of course, the trustworthiness of the field does not imply that scholars are necessarily *right*. They could be wrong for any number of reasons—and it is important that you reason about their conclusions and their evidence, their interpretations and the context, the assumptions they make and the alternatives they ignore. They *are*, however, the best source you are likely to find. Moreover, if they are later shown to *be* wrong, it will most likely be by a member of the same community of critically thinking historians and Biblical scholars.

The same can be said for just about any topic, no matter how controversial or personal. In fact, the more important a topic is in your life, the more important it is to take a course in it, to read a textbook in the area. Here is a brief list of topics that are important to many people, and those people would benefit tremendously by consulting and taking seriously the discipline's findings and viewpoints.

- dieting
- healthy attitudes toward death and dying
- the status of the environment
- causes of crime in the United States
- global warming
- the Arab-Israeli conflict
- what to do about chronic back pain
- cloning

One of the things disciplines often do is contradict common sense. If that happens, you should feel a need to question the common sense. Disciplines are full of carefully amassed evidence, reasoned argumentation, and critiques by others. Common sense is not subject to any of these, certainly not in any systematic way. It is not common sense that the desk you are sitting at is 99 percent empty space; that being cold and wet has nothing to do with catching cold; that ulcers are caused by bacteria, not stress; that though it is unhealthy to keep anger bottled up inside, it is also unhealthy to let it out; that, objectively, there is no such thing as color; that the vast majority of us are capable of acting as the Serbs did in Bosnia. Though these examples contradict most people's common sense, all, according to the most complete evidence we have, are clearly true.

- explanations of near-death experiences
- the morality of abortion, the rights of animals, sexual morality
- the success of economic policies during the Reagan era
- the Vietnam conflict
- U.S. intervention in Somalia
- the efficacy of herbal remedies
- the litigious nature of our society
- parapsychology, telekinesis

When You Disagree

There may be inaccuracies in your text or in lectures. That is quite possible. But you should be wary of concluding too quickly that lectures or texts are inaccurate or biased. If what the book says is contrary to your own experience, there are a number of questions you should carefully consider before concluding that the text is off-base. For example:

- Did I understand clearly what was said?
- Do I understand what the text means, in context?
- Is my disagreement based on common sense? What is the real evidence for the common-sense view?

- Is my own experience limited? Or is it applicable only in one area?
- Do I have a vested interest in disbelieving what is in the text? Is my ego bound up with accepting one view over another?
- Do I feel some fear I may be unaware of at having my world view shaken up? Do the findings in the discipline make me angry?

CHAPTER 2 Exercises

The exercises contain examples from a wide variety of disciplines, including textbooks. Few of these examples will be in the subject you are studying. But *what* the exercises ask you to do *is* directly relevant to the field you are studying. The exercises were chosen because they bring home important points about critical thinking in *any* field.

If possible, after answering the question as it stands, see if you can adapt it to the discipline you are studying.

2.1 Read and then reflect on the following paragraph using some of the questions from the box on p. 47.

> Many sellers make the mistake of paying more attention to the specific products they offer than to the benefits produced by these products. They see themselves as selling a product rather than providing a solution to a need. A manufacturer of drill bits may think that the customer needs a drill bit, but what the customer *really* needs is a hole. These sellers may suffer from "marketing myopia"—they are so taken with their products that they focus only on existing wants and lose sight of underlying customer needs. They forget that a product is only a tool to solve a consumer problem. These sellers will have trouble if a new product comes along that serves the customer's need better or less expensively. The customer with the same *need* will *want* the new product.[13]

- What are the implications of this paragraph for sellers of products? As the field of marketing makes clear, when you have an occupation, you are selling a product: your services. What implications does this paragraph have for *you*?
- In your own words, describe how the author of this paragraph is *reasoning*. That is, don't simply describe the points he is making; rather, describe how he reasons from one point to another.

■ Though the paragraph is presented in a clear and streamlined way, what complications arise?

 2.2 Here are two paragraphs from a composition text:

> Whenever you write, your goal is to communicate effectively with the people who are going to read what you write. These readers are considered your audience. Sometimes your audience might include specific people such as your classmates, your instructor, your friends, your family, or your boss. At other times, you might be writing for the general public that reads your local newspaper.
>
> As you write, ask yourself: Who is going to read this? How much do they already know about my topic? What are their attitudes about my topic? The answers to these questions can help you identify your audience. . . . Once you have analyzed your audience, you will be better able to decide on the content, vocabulary, and tone that are most suitable for your paper.[14]

a. Describe the reasoning in these paragraphs. That is, describe how the authors reason from point to point in the two paragraphs.

b. Do the same kind of analysis with different paragraphs from the readings in your course.

2.3 Write down five questions you have about the discipline you are studying. They should be good questions, so search for some questions where learning the answer is important to you.

2.4 Some archaeologists claim that, because of the ice sheet, humans could not have crossed from Siberia to Alaska earlier than 13,000 years ago. But we know from remains that there were humans all the way at the tip of South America 11,000 years ago. That's 10,000 miles away! Obviously, people could not travel that far across mountains, deserts, and jungles in such a short period of time. So the archaeologists must be wrong: either humans arrived in Alaska earlier, or else humans arrived in South America from someplace else (maybe China).

Can you follow the reasoning in this paragraph? Does it make sense?

2.5 Critical thinking is authentic. Consider math problems. Students often prefer certain math problems because all they have to do is the computations or the calculator work. They hate word problems. That's natural. Computations have a much safer feel to them because you have a good idea of how to proceed. The problem does not look so open-ended. Critical thinking, however, applies to real life problems with a quantitative aspect. Think them through mathematically, and only then do the computation or calculator work. That's what was involved in Exercise 2.4. You had to notice that math was relevant. Once you notice that, the computation is simple.

A Taco Bell sells three tacos and a large drink for $3.36, or you can buy the same items in a "#9 Combo" for $3.38. They seem to have almost a contempt for our ability to think mathematically. A Walgreen's sells microwave popcorn at 49¢ per packet—or a box of three packets for $1.69.

Having any realistic understanding of math shows that buying lottery tickets makes no sense at all. People in math often call lotteries "the stupidity tax." Compare that to taking the ACT: You know that if you answer the questions according to what you know, you'll get many of them wrong. *But*, if you mark the answer sheet at random (as in a lottery), there's a chance you might get a *perfect score*. So, should you mark answers at random when you take standardized tests?

What are some areas of your life where you need to think mathematically?

2.6 Logic of a field. What is the difference between thinking ethically and thinking legally? Give some examples to illustrate the difference.

2.7 Vocabulary of the discipline. As the course goes along, keep a log of terms you can define but still don't really understand. Keep a log of vocabulary words in the field that you can apply directly to your life as you live it now.

2.8 Here are the headings for the seven main parts of a business text.[15]

Part 1. Introducing the World of Business

Part 2. Understanding the Contemporary Business Environment

Part 3. The Business of Managing

Part 4. Understanding People in Organizations

Part 5. Managing Operations and Information

Part 6. Understanding Principles of Marketing

Part 7. Understanding Financial Issues

Make a concept map of the f&p concepts for this course.

2.9 **Group work.** In groups of four, critically discuss the central question of the course. Try to come to a consensus on what it is, how it unifies the course as a whole, how it fits in with the central questions of other related fields.

2.10 Formulate a mission statement for yourself. It should take into account what you believe is most important for you to be doing in your life. Alternatively, formulate a mission statement for yourself as a student in this course.

2.11 Construct your own pre-test and post-test on critical thinking in a subject matter. Choose an important question in the course. It may not be the central question, but it should be very important. Here are some examples:

Life sciences: How does the body work?

Education: How do children learn?

Geology: How do landforms come about?

Business: How does one manage a business?

Composition: How does someone write a good argumentative essay?

Write out an answer to this near the beginning of the course. You will be thinking it out as you compose your response. When your answer is written, put it away somewhere, and don't refer back to it. Give it time to sink into the background. Then, near the end of the course (and without looking at your first answer), write out an answer to the same question.

Then compare the two, but not just with respect to the information each contains (this will obviously increase substantially by the time the semester is over). Compare them with respect to

- how you have organized the information
- how well you have grasped the logic of the answer
- how well you are able to see the parts working together as a whole (synthesis)

You should also notice a marked improvement in the accuracy, importance, precision, and depth of your response.

2.12 As a study skill, memorizing does not work very well. What can you do instead?

2.13 Draw a concept map of critical thinking as you understand it so far.

2.14 Here is a concept map based on a new management paradigm in a management textbook:[16]

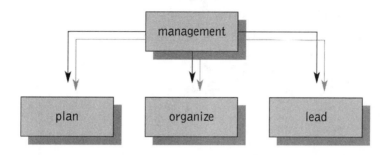

By thinking of *the logic of* this paradigm, can you see what is *missing* as an f&p concept?

2.15 Impediments. Take each of the impediments listed in Chapter 1 (pp. 21–32) and give an original example of how each might be an impediment to thinking critically in the discipline you are studying in this class. Be specific.

2.16 Why would you (or someone else) think that humans are more fit than dinosaurs?

2.17 Group work. Focus on the background story you have for this course. (This is difficult work.)

Individually, take five of the most important concepts in the field. (A good place to get them is from the headings in the table of contents in the text.) Before you read anything about them in the book, write down your main ideas about them: how you understand them, how they work. For example, suppose it is a course in sociology and one of the chapters is entitled Cultural Diversity. Explain what cultural diversity is, how it works, how it comes about, what effects it has, how you feel about it—whatever seems important to you. (Notice that this is an ill-defined question. You'll have to adapt it to your field.)

Now, discuss your responses in groups of four. Your aim in this is not to argue your points with others. It is to formulate a clear statement of the background story that is operating in you.

Next, read the book and compare your story with the account in the book. Discuss this with the same group of four people. But your goal is not to find out if you were right or wrong. It is still to get a conscious grasp of your background story or logic, and to compare it to the logic of the discipline you are studying.

2.18 "We don't really know if the sun will rise tomorrow." Evaluate this statement.

2.19 Group work. Apply the template on pp. 37–38 to an important topic from this chapter.

The Elements of Reasoning

Critical thinking is not the same as thinking. Thinking is a process that involves drawing conclusions about something, forming concepts, making decisions, and having a point of view. It's any activity in which you process things with your mind. So, forming a closely reasoned judgment after paying close attention to the evidence is an example of thinking. But so is jumping to a conclusion without considering any evidence. Similarly, weighing both sides of an issue and carefully checking for biases that might unfairly influence a decision is an example of thinking. But so is stubbornly holding on to prejudices and using stereotypes to judge people.

Although all four descriptions are examples of thinking and reasoning, only the first and third are examples of *critical* thinking. Two conditions are necessary if thinking is to be critical thinking.

First, the thinking has to be reflective; it has to involve thinking-about-my-thinking. Second, this reflective thinking must meet high standards; it must be reflective reasoning that is done well.

This chapter focuses on the elements of our thinking. When we reflect on our thinking, the elements are what we reflect *about*.

The Nuts and Bolts of Critical Thinking

There are at least two or three dozen basic concepts in critical thinking, maybe as many as 50. The most central concepts number around twenty and can be grouped into eight categories. These are called *the elements of reasoning.*

Some of these concepts map out very different aspects of critical thinking; some overlap and are closely related to one another. Being able to think critically means being able to use these elements as tools in our thinking—being able to use them with sensitivity and the knowledge of how they interact. Using them with the standards described in Chapter 4, you can produce thinking that is reliable and trustworthy (though not infallible).

Let's look briefly at an example of an element: *conclusions.* This is a central concept of critical thinking. The idea is that when we reason, we draw conclusions. We want to draw *reasonable* conclusions, not *unreasonable* ones. That is, we want to draw conclusions that are *accurate*, with *sufficient* evidence to back them up, conclusions that are *relevant* to the issue we are investigating. (Accuracy, sufficiency, and relevance are *standards* for using the element *conclusions.*)

Notice how thinking in terms of *conclusions* changes our thinking, makes it more reflective, more critical. It starts to lead us logically from step to step. Someone says something and you realize, "That's a conclusion." Once you realize that, you are led to the next question, "Well, since it's a conclusion, what is it based on?" When you ask that, you don't necessarily mean to be skeptical. The conclusion might be based on excellent evidence. But calling it a conclusion brings home the idea that it's not an absolute, not a given. It is a result of human reasoning, and it is based on some evidence. Now, that leads you to two more questions: "Well, since it's a conclusion based on evidence, is the evidence it's based on accurate?" and "Is the evidence it's based on *enough* evidence to support this conclusion?" Just thinking it out this far puts you deep in the process of critical thinking.

The Elements of Reasoning

Figure 3.1 is a chart of the elements of reasoning.[1] (Compare it to the overview in Figure 1.3 on p. 39.)

Each of the eight wedges shown in Figure 3.1 is an element of reasoning. Whenever we reason through anything, all eight are always present. The "always" is important because it means that in any piece of reasoning, you can reflect on any or all of those eight and be assured of finding them there.

In addition to the eight elements, the chart also contains *context* and *alternatives*. *Context* is the background to the reasoning rather than being literally an element in it, and *alternatives* encompasses the different choices that could be made in the reasoning. Whenever we reason through anything, there is always a context in which it takes place, and there are alternatives that shape it.

The eight elements plus context and alternatives are called the 8+ elements. They are arranged in a circle, but not numbered because there's no required order to them. The order in which it is most beneficial to apply them depends on the question being addressed.

FIGURE 3.1   *The circle of elements.*

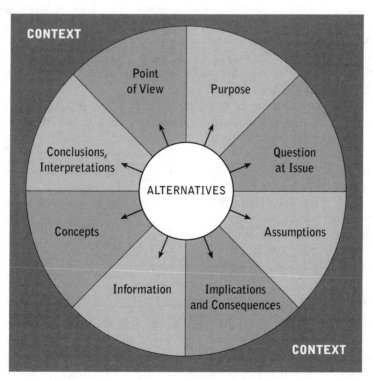

For each of the 8+ elements this book will be saying roughly the same three kinds of thing. It will first introduce the element and try to give a sense of how that element is present in all our reasoning. Second, it will illustrate how identifying that element in many contexts is essential to thinking critically through something. Third, it will describe briefly a number of other critical thinking activities that center around that element.

The initial description of each element is abstract, and for that reason it may be hard to follow, but afterward examples are provided to make the abstract more concrete. As the abstract presentation proceeds, try to get a feel for each element, for its flexibility and usefulness. Each of the elements is essential, and each can furnish us with insight into the heart of the subject we are reasoning about.

Purpose (objectives, goals, desired outcome, function)

Whenever we reason, we do so with a purpose. Therefore, it's always relevant to ask, "What is your *purpose* in that reasoning?" This holds for *any* piece of reasoning. If you read an essay by an author, a good question to ask is, "What is the author's purpose in that essay?" If you perform an experiment, you should ask, "What is the purpose of the experiment?" When a teacher gives a homework assignment, or you write a term-paper, or read a case study, or learn a new procedure for treating a patient with diabetes, it's always relevant and central to ask: What is the purpose of that assignment? What are my goals in writing this paper? Why was this case study presented? What are the objectives behind using this procedure—and how do those objectives fit in with the overall purpose of treating diabetes?

All these examples have to do with *identifying* a purpose in something. But the concept of purpose has other uses. You can not only identify your purpose, but *keep it firmly in mind* as you plow through a whole host of details. That's difficult to do, seeing the forest while looking at the trees. You can *question your purpose*, or an author's purpose, asking whether it is worth achieving, and at what cost. You can have many purposes behind a decision, and you can *prioritize* them, figuring out which goals are most important.

Thus, *purpose*, as an element, serves as a center for asking a host of relevant, reflective questions, as well as for performing a large number of higher-order thinking activities.

Question at Issue (problem, topic, "the point," "q at i")

Whenever we reason through something, there is some question we are trying to answer, some problem we are addressing. So in any act of reasoning, it always makes good sense to ask, "What is the question at issue? What is the problem you are addressing?"

If *purpose* is what you are trying to accomplish, the question at issue (q at i) is the more specific question you are addressing in order to achieve that purpose. The *purpose* of this book, for example, is to be a guide that will help people think their way critically through a subject. By contrast, the *q at i* is: What is the best way to help people accomplish that?

Since all reasoning is about some question, it's always relevant to ask what *is* the question being addressed. What is the question at issue this author is addressing? What, specifically, is the problem being addressed in this piece of art criticism? What are the major questions at issue in this empirical test, in this math problem, in this marketing strategy, in this physical education exercise? What is the question at issue I am addressing in writing this term paper? Questions are vital to all critical thinking. The central question of a course is vital to critical thinking in a discipline.

Notice all the different activities connected to the q at i. You can identify it in different contexts (as in the previous paragraph). After you identify someone's q at i, you might need to go further and ask, "What *other* questions at issue *should* they be addressing? What major questions have they left out?" If you identify the q at i in a term paper, you also want to be mindful and *stay focused* on that question all the way through. If you and I are having a disagreement, I may well want to ask, "How does the question *I* am addressing fit in with the question *you* are addressing?" A good proactive question to ask is, "If I try to solve this problem this way, what further problems are likely to arise?"

All of these are rich ways to explore your thinking and the thinking of others, and all of them revolve around the element *q at i*. As with each of the elements, to learn how to answer questions like these is to develop a range of higher-order thinking skills.

Assumptions (background theory, what is given or taken for granted, axioms)

Whenever you reason through something, you always have to begin somewhere. You can't "begin at the beginning," because there *is* no beginning. What you begin with are your assumptions. Your assumptions consist of everything you take for granted when you think through something. Sometimes people can state their assumptions up front. More often, though, the most crucial assumptions we make are those that are *unstated*. In fact, it is often a major insight to identify assumptions an author may be unaware of even though they underlie his or her reasoning.

Any area where reasoning is taking place is an area where it is important to identify assumptions. If you are having an argument with your friends, maybe a heated argument, a good question to ask is, "What are their main assumptions?" But it is at least as important to ask, "What are *my own* assumptions?"—and to hold yourself to the same standards you apply to your friends.

If you're doing a writing assignment, it's crucial to ask, "What assumptions am I making about the person who will read this?" Whether you ask this question or not, you automatically *do* make assumptions about the reader. The critical thinking question is not whether you *make* assumptions— we all do that all the time. The critical thinking question is whether you are *aware* of the assumptions you're making. Only by becoming aware of your assumptions can you then evaluate them, so that you can be more in charge of your thinking.

Throughout your thinking within a subject, you need to be engaged in actively identifying assumptions. What assumptions is this author making? What assumptions was this sculptor making in her use of materials? What assumptions was Milgram making in the way he interpreted his famous experiment? What assumptions am I making in designing a health plan for this patient?

All the topics so far have been about *identifying* assumptions, but there are any number of other ways you can reflect critically on assumptions. Not only can you identify an author's assumptions, you can also *compare* them to your own or to other people's assumptions; you can *evaluate* them in the light of evidence. You can put people's assumptions (including your own) in a larger context, asking how they are rooted in their upbringing or their cultural background. You can "try on" certain assumptions, tracing out what their implications would be if you really believed them. You can seek out others with different assumptions as a way of becoming more aware of your own.

Assumptions, then, like all the elements, serve as a core idea around which to investigate a large number of critical thinking questions.

Sometimes we are told, "Never make assumptions," "Don't assume anything," or "When you ASSUME, you make an ASS of U and ME. So don't assume."

But that advice is incoherent. We *have to* make assumptions. The speaker of the advice above is *assuming* that the hearers follow the play on words, that they care, that advice can help, etc. It is *impossible* to avoid making assumptions.

We don't need to stop making assumptions, we need to make *reasonable* assumptions.

Implications and Consequences
(what follows, costs and benefits)

Just as your reasoning has to begin somewhere, it also has to end somewhere. The area *beyond* where it ends constitutes the implications and consequences of your reasoning. To ask about the implications and consequences of a piece of reasoning is to ask "What *follows* from it?" If you have a certain position on capital punishment, you want to ask, "What are the implications of that position?" That is, what further things must I adhere to if I hold that position? What further beliefs does this commit me to?

If you make a decision, you need to ask, "What will be the consequences, both positive and negative, of making this decision rather than that one?" Interpreting a case study has implications for how you interpret other case studies. Designing a social studies experiment, creating innovative management plans, constructing a schedule of activities for middle-school students, reacting in a certain way when people get angry at you—all of these have implications and consequences, and all have different implications and consequences from alternative designs, plans, and schedules you could have used instead, from different reactions you could have had. It is important to identify implications and consequences in each of these cases.

But to think critically, you need to become skillful at handling implications and consequences in ways that go beyond simply identifying them. In most real-world situations, for example, consequences are seldom automatic, so you need to do something more subtle: not just identify consequences of an action, but assess the *likelihood* of various possible consequences, none of which is certain. Similarly, because many decisions have both a plus-side and a minus-side, you need to be able to *weigh* the costs and benefits of various consequences.

Focusing on the element of *implications and consequences* allows you to see aspects of situations and thought processes that, previously, you saw only occasionally—in a hit-or-miss sort of way. The element allows you to focus on something that is one of the keys to reasoning well, to taking charge of your thinking.

Each of the elements in fact functions in this way. As you get better at internalizing them and using them, they will make changes in how you think about your life as well as about the subject matter you are studying in school.

Information (data, evidence, observations)

Whenever you reason, you use information. Therefore, it's always relevant to ask, "What information pertains to this issue?" You might ask, "What information do I have, and what information do I not have, but *need?"* "What information does the author of this article supply? What information does this author omit?" "What data does this experiment yield?" "What evidence do I have to back up my claim?" "What do you observe about these cells in the microscope?" "What do you observe about the children in this special education setting?"

Notice that people use information even when they reason badly through an issue. People who draw prejudiced conclusions often base their reasoning on incomplete or incorrect information. So, in addition to *identifying* the information in a piece of reasoning, you need to be able to *evaluate* that information. Standard critical thinking skills include the ability to distinguish information from your interpretation of that information, to decide when you need more information to draw a reasonable conclusion, to know how to find other reliable pieces of information on a topic, to organize information in a coherent way, and to present it clearly.

Information is an essential element of reasoning. But information by itself is seldom enough to decide important issues. We need the other elements of reasoning just as much. If you know some information, but you don't know the implications of that information, you can be seriously misled even by the facts. If you know some information, but you don't know the questions at issue that the information is relevant to, then the information just floats in your memory, like pieces of trivia.

Concepts (organizing ideas, categories)

All reasoning is in terms of concepts. If you are reasoning about democracy in America, you have a concept of *democracy* that is operative in your thinking. It is part of being reflective to ask, "What is my concept of democracy? What is my understanding of that term?" If you are trying to figure out whether an office is running efficiently, it helps to step back from that question and ask, "What is my concept of *efficiency* here? What earmarks do I use to decide whether an office is running efficiently?"

The same is true with less familiar concepts like real numbers, or cognitive dissonance, or iambic pentameter. A major goal of courses in a field is to help students grasp the most important concepts in the field. Teachers and texts often try to accomplish this by means of definitions. Thus, a geology text[2] defines *compound* as "a substance resulting from the bonding of two or more different elements, e.g., water (H_2O) or quartz (SiO_2)." But it's important to realize that the definition is a means to an end, not an end in itself. To grasp it, you must know what "bonding" is, how this process works. Otherwise, you may be just repeating a definition rather than grasping the *concept* the definition refers to. The goal is for the student to internalize the concept of *compound* and to be able to use that concept to think through issues and problems. So a good question to ask yourself about important but unfamiliar terms is, "What is *my understanding* of the concept that term represents?"

One helpful way to look at concepts is to describe them using a word or a term rather than a sentence. Thus, *honesty* is a concept, whereas "Honesty is the best policy" is an *assumption* rather than a concept. *The Treaty of Versailles* is a concept (of course it is also an object), whereas "The Treaty of Versailles formed the peace terms of World War I" is a piece of information rather than a concept. Why is that important? Because that is the feature that allows concepts to be so versatile, to be usable in a wide variety of contexts. You can use the concepts of *honesty* or *the Treaty of Versailles* to think through hundreds of important problems. The sentences containing these concepts, on the other hand, are far more specific and therefore usable in a much more limited set of contexts.

It is a considerable skill to learn to identify the main concepts in our reasoning. It is very similar to identifying assumptions, and it is difficult in much the same way. Just as we take our assumptions for granted, we take our concepts for granted also. If I have the inner conviction that I've been treated unfairly, it doesn't often lead me to ask, "What *is* my concept of fairness? What do I mean when I classify this action as unfair?" For example, I can *feel* an action to be unfair simply when I've been hurt by it. If I don't then go on to explore the *concept of fairness* that is at work in my reaction, I may continue to draw the conclusion that I've been unfairly treated even when it is just bad luck.

Notice again that concepts are always present in our thinking. Every single thought you have is guided by concepts. The question for the critical thinker then is not whether you are using concepts, but whether you are *aware* of the concepts you're using.

Conclusions, Interpretations (inferences, solutions, decisions arrived at)

To think about the world you live in is to interpret it, to draw conclusions about it. So it's always relevant to ask, "How are you interpreting this situation, this poem, this philosophical issue, this equation, this anything? What conclusions are you drawing? What conclusion is this author drawing?"

It is often vitally important in critical thinking to distinguish information from someone's *interpretation* of that information. We see people's faces (information) and we interpret the look we see there as anger, maybe as anger at *us*. But we can easily be mistaken in that *conclusion*. The person may be feeling sad or tired rather than angry, or the person may indeed be angry, but at something that has nothing whatsoever to do with us. People who diagnose patients need to be constantly aware of the information they are receiving about the patient and of their interpretation of that information. They then need to reflect on their interpretation and question whether alternative interpretations are more plausible. That's true of diagnosing patients, but it's equally true of office managers trying to diagnose problems; or students "diagnosing" study habits that work well for some courses but not for others; or technicians sitting at a radar screen interpreting blips.

In addition to the ability to identify interpretations and conclusions, to be an effective critical thinker you need to develop other skills centering around this element. After you've given your interpretation of a situation, for example, you should be able to compare your interpretation with the interpretations of others and try to decide which is most reasonable (or recognize the equal legitimacy of different interpretations). You need to be able to contextualize interpretations, too, because the distinction between information and interpretation depends heavily on context: When a beginner looks through a microscope, the data might be the fuzzy orangish blob she sees, and the interpretation might be that it is a cell. For a more advanced practitioner, the data might be that she sees a cell, pure and simple, and the interpretation might be that the cell is beginning to undergo mitosis.

It is often necessary to group a set of interpretations to see how they all follow from an underlying background system. For example, evolutionary biologists interpret the hibernation of bears, the day-long lifespan of a mayfly, or the shape and size of a palm frond—indeed, almost all plant and animal characteristics—in terms of how that characteristic increases the organism's chances at reproductive success.

Point of View (frame of reference, perspective)

Whenever we reason through something, we do so within some point of view. So it always makes sense to ask, "From what point of view are you addressing this issue?" To call *point of view* an element of reasoning is to assert that there is no such thing as "point-of-view-less" reasoning. *All* reasoning occurs within some point of view. Addressing the same question from a different point of view can produce a whole different set of purposes, assumptions, conclusions, and so on.

It is sometimes difficult to distinguish point of view from assumptions. Indeed, the two often overlap. For example, to have a conservative's point of view on a political issue is to make certain assumptions about the importance of promoting free enterprise and reducing the role of government. But point of view is often quite distinct from assumptions. For example, consider *physical* point of view: While you are reading these words your point of view is physically different from that of anyone around you. You, physically, are viewing this page at a certain angle; everyone else is looking at other things: their own books, at a teacher, out a window. But in the uniqueness of your physical point of view there is no assumption that one is better than another. They are simply different points of view. There are also *psychological* points of view. If you write your name in the blanks below, you'll end up with an accurate (and sometimes profound) sentence:

_____ is at the *center* of my point of view. Everything I think about is from the point of view of _____'s mind.

However, even though you are obviously at the center of all your thoughts, that does not mean that you assume your point of view is more valid than other people's. Seeing things from your own point of view does not automatically make you egocentric. (Of course, some arrogant people *may* assume their own point of view is automatically more valid, but making the assumption is different from having the point of view.)

At least one point of view is distinctly relevant to the course you are taking, and that is the point of view of the discipline itself. If it's a course in sociology, you will be expected to address most questions from a sociological point of view—not, usually, from a biological, religious, personal, business, or even an ethical point of view. These may be relevant, and they may well be extremely important. But they are *different* points of view from a purely sociological one. It is important to think about sociological findings from an ethical point of view. In many cases, sociologists contend that an ethical perspective should in fact take priority over a sociological one. However, the two points of view are distinct—and you should be able to think in terms of either. Learning to think from the point of view of a discipline is one of the most valuable outcomes a course in the discipline can provide. The goal of a course is not simply to provide you with new facts to fit into your old point of view; it is to provide you with new perspectives, fresh and reputable points of view that you can use to see things in a way you couldn't before.

That is not the end of the matter, however. To think through important questions in a field often requires you to look at the question from the point of view of other related disciplines as well. Seeing biological problems from a biochemical perspective is often illuminating. Looking at a human-interaction problem from a psychological *and* a sociological *and* a historical point of view provides insight that a single perspective will not yield. Part of being a critical thinker is the ability to bring to bear a variety of relevant points of view. This is addressed directly in multidisciplinary courses, which explicitly require thinking from the points of view of several disciplines. But identifying multidisciplinary points of view is valuable even within a course in a single discipline.

In addition to *identifying* points of view, you need to develop other related skills. Sometimes, for instance, it's difficult to zero in on the point of view you are reasoning from. You can make your point of view clearer by presenting it in the context of other competing points of view. You can say what a sociological point of view is more clearly by distinguishing it from, say, a psychological one. If you are considering a nursing diagnosis on a patient, you can contrast your nursing point of view with the *patient's* point of view—also with the doctor's, the hospital's, the patient's family's, the HMO's. Some of these are *always* relevant. Others are relevant in one case but not in another.

Similarly, a major critical thinking skill to develop is the ability to *evaluate* points of view. Clearly it is not enough just to know what my point of view is. Bigots, for example, will sometimes openly admit that they look at things from a bigoted point of view. They sometimes even seem proud of it. Obviously, that is not an example of critical thinking. Once I've identified a point of view on an issue, my own or anyone's, I need to evaluate how plausible it is, how much it fits the evidence, how biased it is.

Alternatives (other possibilities, options, choices)

Whenever you reason, there are alternatives. One of the great benefits of learning to think critically is that you gain the freedom of having alternatives to your normal ways of approaching things. The search for alternatives fits with each of the elements. If you have a purpose, you should ask, "What alternative purpose should I be trying to accomplish instead?" or "What other purpose can I accomplish *in addition?*" If you are reasoning through a question at issue, you can ask, "What *other* questions at issue should I be considering?" Similarly, "What alternative assumptions could I make?" "What other consequences are there of this decision besides the ones I've noticed?" "What other sources of information could I use?" "What are some alternative ways of understanding this key concept?" "What are other possible interpretations of this person's actions, this text, this experiment?" "What other conclusions could I come to?" "What other points of view are relevant with respect to this issue?"

Each of the elements of reasoning is empowering, but thinking about the elements in terms of *alternatives* is empowering in a more direct way. *Thinking outside the box* is envisioning alternatives where before there seemed to be only the sides of the box. Getting in the habit of searching for alternatives allows us to see many potential paths ahead of us, where before there seemed to be only one. Both psychologically and practically, this is empowering. Within a subject matter, it's equally empowering. There are alternative ways of reasoning through experiments, health-care issues, information systems, or business problems—through anything. Math teachers used to teach that there was only one right answer to a math problem and that there was only one correct way to solve it. Though many math problems do have only one answer, there are always alternative ways to come to that answer, alternative ways to reason through it.

For many people, simply *seeing* alternatives (where there seemed to be none before) opens paths for them, puts doors in the sides of the box. But, in addition to identifying alternatives, you need to be able to think your way down alternative possible paths, and then compare them before deciding which path is the best one to follow. Another ability you should cultivate with alternatives is the ability to live with the ambiguity of realizing that there are multiple paths to follow. Sometimes you need to be able to *combine* alternatives, seeing how a third possibility allows you to accomplish both of two seemingly irreconcilable alternatives.

For example, it often seems as though we have to choose: either fight for our own point of view or give in to the other person's. There are, however, usually alternatives that are different from either choice: discuss the issue; ask for what we need (rather than demanding it); compromise; find the good in the other person's point of view; take turns; seek arbitration; let the other person prevail, but do so out of generosity rather than giving in.

There is also something else to live with once you start taking alternatives seriously. In all major events in your life or in your thinking, there are likely to be alternative reasonable paths to follow, and each one will have its own consequences, both positive and negative. Therefore, it is unusual for any one path to accomplish all you wish for. If you choose to major in English, you give up other fields you may well be interested in. If you have a long-term relationship with X, even when you find a good deal of happiness, you automatically give up other possible futures. When doctors operate on patients unsuccessfully, the consciousness that there were other paths they could have followed can be a source of deep guilt (even if they chose the one that was most reasonable beforehand). It might be nice if we didn't feel guilt or regret or the loss of other directions our life might have taken, but that's not the way our minds work. We humans *do* have such feelings. And telling ourselves that we *shouldn't* feel what we in fact *do* feel is simply unreasonable—both because it's unproductive and because it involves denying reality. So we need to develop the ability—one that involves emotions in a strong way—to give up desired alternative paths, accepting the fact that it's often appropriate to grieve for paths we could not follow.

Context (setting, background)

We do not reason in a vacuum. Our reasoning always takes place in a context, and the question at issue always exists within that context. So it's always relevant to ask, "What is the context in which this reasoning is being done?" Writing, for example, is obviously always done in a context. If you're reading a book, it may be relevant to ask, "When was this written? In what language? With what cultural or historical background? What was going on at the time it was written?" Other questions may be important: "How old is the writer? What was going on in his or her personal life?" A favorite question of some deconstructionists is, "How does the context of the writing make the writer *not* address certain questions?"

What is the context in which a drama is performed, an experiment carried out? What is the setting in which a managerial decision must be made?

In textbooks, problems are often given without a context. A problem might state the cooling capacity of air-conditioning systems and the cubic footage of a room to be air-conditioned, and ask you to find the size of the AC unit needed to cool that room. In real life, such a problem would have a context that might need to be taken into account: window area, number of shade trees, intensity of sunlight in that climate, room dividers, wall insulation. In a textbook, the context is that of a school problem: the book asks you to ignore all complicating factors and to act as if the only relevant factors are the ones stated. That is one reason why learning in a field is so difficult to transfer to real-life problems, which are usually much more complicated and less certain.

The following is a list of some of the main contexts that you may need to consider when reasoning through a particular question:

- historical
- economic
- cultural
- linguistic
- scientific
- personal
- social

Sometimes one aspect of a context is crucial for understanding a problem, while in another problem that same kind of context is irrelevant. It would be irrelevant to trace the history of air conditioning systems as part of answering the question about cooling a room.

This completes the quick survey of the 8+ elements from the circle shown in Figure 3.1. A major part of critical thinking is to *go around the circle*; that is, analyze a question, problem, or topic in terms of the 8+ elements and synthesize them to see the logic of how they fit together.

Three Additional Elements of Reasoning

Three other elements must be mentioned. They are not explicitly in the circle because they overlap categories. Still, they are important concepts in critical thinking.

Reasons

Reasoning can be defined as drawing conclusions on the basis of reasons. So, reasons are always present when someone is reasoning. It's crucially important to identify reasons: "What reasons do I have for my beliefs on this issue?" "What reasons does this author give for her conclusions?"

Reasons is a much broader category than the other elements of reasoning. Reasons can include pieces of *information, assumptions,* and *interpretations* and *conclusions* someone has come to on other grounds—almost any of the elements.

Claims (judgments)

People who teach courses specifically on critical thinking tend to emphasize the word "claim" a great deal, and it's a useful term to get in the habit of using. It is a very general word. It has roughly the same meaning as the term *judgment,* or *statement.* The terms *claim* and *judgment* overlap all the other elements. When I say, "This is my *purpose,*" "This is the *question at issue,*" "These are the *assumptions* I am making," and so on—all of these are *claims.* People can make claims about anything, and (except for questions and commands) most of what you read and hear consists of claims.

Aristotle says that humans are rational animals—that is, he makes the *claim* that humans are rational animals. Notice how explicitly calling it a claim rather than just describing it as what Aristotle says helps you to think about it in a slightly different way. Calling it a claim holds it up before your mind as something to be wondered about: What reasons did Aristotle have for making that claim? Is it true that humans are rational animals?

To call something a claim does not necessarily call it into question, but it does leave the statement *open* to question. It reminds us that we can ask further questions about the evidence for believing the statement, how to interpret it, and what significance it has. That is why claim and judgment are such useful critical thinking terms.

It should be emphasized that calling something a claim or a judgment does not imply that it is shaky or doubtful. Newton claims that objects moving in a straight line at a steady speed will continue to move that way until acted upon by some external force. That is one of the most well-established claims we know. It is not at all shaky or doubtful. But it is still a *claim,* and calling it that recognizes explicitly that all our beliefs are subject to revision in the light of new evidence.

Hypothesis

The term *hypothesis* is a central part of reasoning in the sciences. It doesn't play such a prominent role in other fields (though perhaps it should). A hypothesis is a type of assumption I make or a conclusion I draw, usually about the way a situation will turn out, but I hold it tentatively while waiting to see whether it will turn out the way I thought it would, waiting to see whether my hypothesis will be confirmed or disconfirmed, often by experimentation.

This is a fairly formal use of the term *hypothesis*, but the truth is that we form hypotheses all the time in our thinking. We may not call them hypotheses, but we make predictions about how things will work out, and then we check to see if they do work out that way. If they do, then we usually conclude we were right; if they don't, we (at least sometimes) conclude that we were wrong.

Being reflective means recognizing the hypotheses that you are making. When you read a novel or watch a movie, you make predictions about what will happen and how characters will change. When you read a textbook attentively, you do the same kind of thing: you have a tentative awareness of where you think the book is heading. When interacting with people, you make hypotheses about what they are feeling. You can have a hypothesis—a very quick one—that the expression on someone's face is one of annoyance. The advantage of calling this a hypothesis is that it *displays* for you the tentative and revisable nature of your interpretation. It directs you to look for further evidence that your interpretation is justified. Similarly, when writing, you make hypotheses about how the reader will understand what you are saying. So, critical writers pay a lot of attention to feedback about their writing because that allows them to refine their writing in the light of whether their hypotheses were confirmed.

We are unaware of most of the hypotheses we make in our day-to-day living. A major part of becoming a critical thinker, however, is becoming aware of how you think. That is the process of reflection. Reflection helps you take control of your habitual patterns of thinking, rather than letting the habitual patterns control you. John Maynard Keynes said, "When somebody persuades me that I am wrong, I change my mind. What do *you* do?"

A Misleading Element: Facts

The term *fact* is not in the list of elements. Facts fall under *information*, but habitually using the word *fact* can do a disservice to critical thinking. Pieces of information that we are very certain about we often call "facts." We believe they have been proved. These are usually pieces of information that seem to us to be completely unproblematic. For

Run your finger down three or four pages in your textbook. Pick out some sentences that are important. (Don't pick incidental statements or mere examples the author is providing.) Describe those sentences to yourself as *facts*. Then describe those sentences to yourself as *claims*. When you describe them as claims, you should notice that you no longer take the statements as absolutes. What questions about those specific sentences arise in your mind when you call them claims?

example, it's a fact that Neil Armstrong was the first person to walk on the moon, that smoking causes lung cancer ("Surgeon General's Warning: Smoking cigarettes causes lung cancer, heart disease, and emphysema, and may complicate pregnancy"), that Michelangelo sculpted the statue *David*, that Lee surrendered at Appomattox, that I like chocolate ice cream, that A got angry when B insulted him. There is nothing automatically uncritical about using the word *fact*, as long as we do it carefully.

Still, it's a term that tends to shut down inquiry rather than promoting it, and it tends to conceal problematic aspects of those claims that are labeled facts. In the previous list of facts, all are (as far as I know) true, but the second, fourth, and sixth facts have something problematic about them. Smoking *does* cause lung cancer, but calling it a "fact" may hide the *statistical* nature of the claim; it does not necessarily mean that everyone who smokes will get the disease, and therefore it cannot be refuted by giving *examples* of people who managed to smoke to a ripe old age. It means that a significant percentage of those who smoke will have a greater chance of developing lung cancer than those who do not smoke. Similarly, it is true that Lee surrendered to Grant at Appomattox, but surrendered *what*? The statement, though true, is *elliptical*: it leaves out an important part and can easily be misleading. Many people draw the conclusion that Lee surrendered the *Confederacy*, but that is not true at all. Similarly, it may be a fact that A got angry when B insulted him. It may be true as far as it goes. However, it may be a *superficial* truth, and therefore misleading. We often get angry at insults because the insult connects with some fear we have about ourselves, often a childhood fear. It may be more beneficial to A for him to realize that B's remark tapped into his own pre-existing fears in some way. But if A calls it a *fact*, he tends to close off further exploration of what is really going on inside him.

It is probably better to think of facts as pieces of information that we assume do not require questioning or clarification in the context of a particular discussion.

How to Analyze a Piece of Reasoning Using the Elements

The reasoning you are trying to understand may be written: an argument, a news story, a chapter from a textbook, a novel, a poem, almost anything. Or the person doing the reasoning may instead be speaking to you. It could be someone you know, or a news analyst on TV. It could be someone you are having a discussion with. The person whose reasoning you are trying to understand may be you.

The point of analysis is to understand, in a fairly deep way, just what the person is saying, how he or she is reasoning through an issue.

The following questions are *guides* only. Sometimes you will have to be flexible and adapt a question to fit the piece of reasoning you are trying to understand. (For example, you may often have to change the singular to the plural, and vice versa. If the questions are phrased one way to understand an argument, you may have to ask them somewhat differently to apply them to a novel or a chapter in the text.) That flexibility is also part of learning to reason well. Sometimes you may need to do an analysis in greater depth and detail, or you may need to focus on different aspects of how the elements enter a piece of reasoning. So some further analysis questions are suggested in parentheses after the basic ones.

Going Around the Circle: The Basic Process of Analysis

1. What is the person's main *purpose* in this piece of reasoning? (What other goals or objectives does the person hope to accomplish in this piece of reasoning?)

2. What is the key *question* or problem the person is addressing? (What are two or three of the most important subsidiary questions at issue?)

3. What is the most important *information* the person is using to reason through this issue? (What other information or data does the person need in this piece of reasoning?)

4. What are the person's major *conclusions*? How is the person *interpreting* this issue? (How does the person answer the main question at issue? What solutions are being offered?)

5. What are the main *concepts* the reasoning depends on? (How does the person understand those concepts? How do those concepts fit together in the person's reasoning?)

6. What are the main *assumptions* the person is making in this piece of reasoning? (What are the crucial unstated assumptions the author is making?)

7. What are the main *implications and consequences* of the person's reasoning? (What are some of the unforeseen consequences of this line of reasoning?)

8. From what *point of view* is the person addressing this question? (What other points of view are necessary to understand this piece of reasoning? What discipline's point of view is being used to address this issue? What other disciplines would help illuminate this reasoning?)

9. What is the *context* of the issue the person is addressing? (What circumstances led up to the issue and to this person's reasoning? What is the background in the discipline [scientific, artistic, cultural, business, sociological, etc.] in which this issue is being addressed?)

10. What *alternatives* are there? (What alternative answers could you reasonably give to the preceding questions? What alternatives are there to the person's reasoning?)

Working with the Elements: The Logic of Something

Becoming a critical thinker means becoming adept at using the elements explicitly and reflectively in your thinking. This involves being able to take a piece of reasoning, your own or someone else's, and analyze it using all 8+ elements from the circle in Figure 3.1. It may seem unrealistic to go through all 8+ elements with respect to every reasoning problem you encounter, but it's a good way to become more proficient in using the elements (and you will quickly get faster at it).

There is another benefit to taking a problem and analyzing it in terms of the 8+ elements. In Chapter 2 you were introduced to the concept of *the logic of*. Going around the circle when dealing with a problem displays the logic of that problem. The elements, after all, are *parts* of a *whole*. Though they are valuable individually, they are even more valuable when you think through a question in terms of how they fit together, in terms of the whole circle. So going around the circle involves not just analysis, but *synthesis* as well: not just breaking an issue down into its component parts, but also seeing it as an integrated whole.

This applies to topics within a discipline as well as to questions in your personal life. Look back to Chapter 2 for an example of someone going around the circle with respect to the discipline itself. Going around the circle is *versatile*: it applies to *any* topic, question, or problem in the discipline. Indeed, a central part of understanding a field is the ability to think through topics like these in a deep and thorough way:

- supply and demand
- how to prepare a speech
- plate tectonics
- the communication process model and its application to marketing
- the problem of how altruism is possible
- the way the concept of "the frontier" has shaped Americans' view of their country.

Similarly, thinking critically about your personal life means that you think through topics like the following in a deep and thorough way:

- taking this course
- how my fears get in the way of my personal growth
- the most effective way for me to study for exams
- why my boss repeatedly takes his anger out on me
- adolescence.

In working through the elements, you may need to adapt the way a particular element fits in with the demands of the question being considered. In the previous lists, the items are described in different forms—questions, concepts, topics, incidents, fragments of a thought process—to emphasize how versatile the circle of elements is. There is no magic formula for how to apply the elements uniformly to any question that arises. Making that adaptation is also part of thinking critically.

Analyzing Positions You Disagree With

Sometimes you will be called on to analyze a position that you disagree with deeply. That's an important part of critical thinking because before you can evaluate a position reasonably, you have to understand

Take some point of view you deeply disagree with:

communism, capitalism

atheism, religion

conservatism, liberalism

Analyze it. Go around the circle. Be sure to analyze it in a fairminded way.

Apply the three tests, especially the second one: An advocate of the point of view (a communist or whatever) should be able to say, "Yes, you have captured it well. That is exactly what I believe in."

it accurately. Here are three quick tests of whether you have given an accurate, fairminded analysis of a view you disagree with.

First, there should be no words of evaluation lurking beneath the surface of your analysis.

Second, a person who holds that position should be able to say, "Yes, you have captured it well. That is exactly what I believe in."

Third, a neutral critical-thinking observer, reading your analysis, should not be able to tell if you agree or disagree with the person's position. If anything, because you have been empathetic in your analysis, the observer's suspicion should be that you advocate the position.

Example: Thinking Through the Logic of Getting Married

Chris and Sean are considering getting married, and Chris tries to think through the question as deeply as possible. [The *italicized* remarks in brackets are a critical thinking commentary on Chris's reasoning.]

■ What is the purpose of marriage?
  - To live as full and as satisfying a life as possible, for both of us.

    [*Notice that this would not be everyone's purpose in getting married. Chris's response did not mention children, for example, and the purpose of marriage for many people includes children. Also, notice that Chris could have listed more purposes, not just that one.*]

■ What is the main question at issue?
  - Should I marry Sean?
  - Should I marry Sean now?

    [*Chris could have asked other questions, and these might influence subsequent answers: Do I love Sean? How can I tell whether marrying Sean would help us live the happy and satisfying life I want. How can I tell this with good reason, not just an unsupported opinion?*]

■ What are the main assumptions I make about marriage?
  - That it's a commitment to monogamy.
  - That marriage is a lifelong commitment.

    [*This assumption leads Chris to identify a different kind of assumption:*]
  - That we will both grow older, and our looks will change.

    [*Chris is not going through the elements mechanically, without thinking, but as part of a process of genuinely thinking through the idea of marrying Sean. Therefore, Chris takes the time to notice an implication of the last assumption: that though how they look*]

*may be important to both of them, it should not be the crucial fac-
tor if marriage is a lifelong commitment and their looks will
change over time.]*

- What are the main implications and consequences of marrying?
  - First, there is the implication already mentioned, that mar-
    riage should not be based too heavily on how we look.
  - There are many legal consequences of marrying someone.
  - Children may or may not be a consequence.

    *[This leads Chris to notice another question at issue: Should
    Sean and I discuss our attitudes toward children (including, maybe,
    adopted children) before we address the question of marriage?]*

  - There will probably be conflicts of interest in the future. In
    fact, there will probably be some *serious* conflicts of interest.
    → It would be especially good to have some psychological
    tools available to deal with these conflicts when they arise.

    *[Chris wonders if the statement about future conflicts of inter-
    est is a* consequence *or an* assumption, *and decides that in a
    way it is both: the conflicts of interest themselves are a conse-
    quence; the claim that there will be such conflicts of interest is
    an assumption.]*

- What information do I have (or need to have) about marrying
  Sean?
  - I have a lot of information about myself: about my likes and
    dislikes, about my long-term goals, about how I see marriage,
    about my religious beliefs, about how I was raised.
  - I have a lot of information about Sean as well, but not near-
    ly as much as I have about myself. → Maybe we should
    talk about this.
  - I have heard that certain kinds of dysfunctionality run in
    families. My father was an alcoholic. I really don't know much
    about Sean's childhood. It would be a good idea to get more
    information about this so that we know how to deal with
    problems stemming from this as they arise in our marriage.
  - I know I have a certain amount of fear about committing to
    marriage. → I assume Sean does too. → We should talk
    about this. We both need more information.

- What are the main concepts I use when I think about marriage?
  - Well, the main one is the concept of *marriage* itself. What is
    my idea of marriage? What is involved in *being married* for
    me? What is Sean's concept of marriage?
  - What is my concept of *loving someone?* My concept of being
    in love? What do I understand by those terms and how
    they apply to us?

- Is *being a friend* part of being married to a person? What do I understand by being a friend?

- One thing I want with the person I marry is to share unconditional love. But what *is* unconditional love? Does that mean that I would love the person *no matter what?* That's an extremely broad commitment, and—once I start imagining possible scenarios—a scary prospect to me. Is it even possible to love people no matter what they do?

[Concepts often influence our behavior below the level of awareness. That is why it's so important to identify the concepts that operate in us. Suppose Chris and Sean had radically different concepts of marriage and were unaware of this. One might have a concept of marriage as, for example, a union that links two whole families, while the other might think of it as being only between two individuals, with their families being completely irrelevant. Because of their different concepts, Sean's behavior with respect to their families might be completely inexplicable to Chris, and vice versa. Both may see their own behavior as entirely appropriate—and the other's behavior as entirely irresponsible.]

- What conclusions should I draw? What interpretations am I using?

[Chris has already come to a number of conclusions while reasoning out the elements so far: the importance of talking about their attitudes toward children, getting some information and tools for conflict resolution, and acknowledging the potential effects of having an alcoholic father. Chris may also be coming to a tentative conclusion (a hypothesis, maybe) that the concept of unconditional love is one that does not apply in marriage.]

  - Whether to get married to Sean or not is the main conclusion I am trying to decide. But there are more specific conclusions and interpretations as well.

  - That Sean is a loving, caring, affectionate individual.

  [Notice that Chris calls this an interpretation, rather than information. Chris's information may be that Sean has acted in a loving, caring, affectionate way before marriage. This is often very different from being a loving, caring, affectionate individual.]

  - That this is the right time for me to consider marriage seriously.

  - That our interests, personalities, and the way we view life are compatible.

- What points of view should I consider?

  - My own, of course: the point of view of someone who has had a certain kind of upbringing, in the society we live in, who has certain expectations and hopes about the future.

- Sean's.
- Are there male and female points of view on marriage?
  → I don't know. Maybe that's just a stereotype.
- Our families' points of view.
- Is it important for me to consider society's point of view, or a legal point of view, or a psychological point of view?

  [It is important to consider other points of view if they are relevant, and if they are likely to give a person insight into the problem being reasoned out. This is often difficult to decide beforehand.]

■ What alternatives are there?
  - Continue as we are now.
  - Decide that marriage is not in the cards for us.
  - My Al-Anon book talks about not forcing solutions: "Instead of redoubling my effort, I can slow down and reassess the situation."[3] That seems reasonable under the circumstances. So we could defer the decision to the beginning of next year when some of the uncertainties in our lives will, I hope, be sorted out a little.
  - Consciously decide to enter into some new relationship with one another. → Each of these brings up a host of new possibilities, and new feelings as well. → Those are all alternatives to the main question at issue I'm addressing. But there are also alternatives to the other elements I've just gone through:
  - I've thought a lot about my concept of marriage, and the legal point of view just entered my mind. Does my concept of marriage automatically bring with it the idea of legality? → Could we have a relationship with one another that we would consider being married, even if it was not *legally* binding?
  - An alternative source of information: I should buy a good book that deals with the decision to get married. I know I can't learn everything I need to know from a book, but I don't want to be afraid to consult books either, especially about such an important decision. I can probably learn some things I haven't considered at all. And all I stand to lose is a little time.

    [Chris could also have considered alternative purposes, consequences, interpretations, and so on.]

■ In what context is this question being addressed?
  - Well, it's a real context for me. It's not a problem in a textbook where filling in an answer merely results in a grade. This is my life I'm talking about. If I don't carefully consid-

er the important parts of the decision to get married, it may have an impact on the rest of my life.

- There is the context of where we are in our relationship, how long we've been together, our ages and backgrounds, the influence of friends, family, and society (and some influences I may not even be aware of).
- Should I have addressed context first, before I did any of the other elements?

[Remember, there is no right order to apply the elements. The order that is most useful may vary from question to question. Many people have the experience that no matter which one they start with, it feels as if they should have done another one first. It often helps to describe the context at the beginning, so that we are sure to anchor the problem in its actual setting and not let it become an abstract puzzle.]

Context, purpose, and question at issue are often good places to start. So is point of view, for example when you are reasoning within the point of view of a particular discipline. On the other hand, alternatives is one that should be kept in mind as you go through each element. It is good to revisit *alternatives* at the end of your analysis to open up new insights that you may have overlooked.

Trusting the Process

You may have a number of concerns as you finish Chapter 3, particularly if you have tried to work through the elements in the subject you are studying. You may be concerned with how the elements fit together. You may see that they sometimes overlap, that their application is not always completely clear, that what you thought was an *assumption* may be an *implication* or a *point of view* in another context. You may find yourself concluding from concerns like these that the elements are confusing. These are natural concerns. They are a part of many people's reactions.

A good thing to do is give the elements a chance to develop in you. Trust the process. You don't have to trust it completely, but you should give it a chance to take hold. The benefits start to come when you get familiar enough with the elements to use them in your day-to-day practice of thinking, both inside the course and out. That takes some time. You should expect to feel some resistance inside you. Most of us have a strong propensity to continue down more familiar paths, ones that seem safer. It will probably feel unsafe to have your thinking process slowed and broken into parts. It will likely feel unsafe to face the multitude of questions and doubts that may arise as you go through this process.

These beginning exercises will help you become familiar with going around the circle of elements.

3.1 Choose some problem or question you have. It can be in the field you're studying, but it may be better to begin with one from your personal life.

Think through each of the elements with respect to the problem or question you have chosen. Go around the circle as Chris did with respect to marrying Sean.

(It is best to begin with a problem that's familiar to you and not too difficult. The purpose is to become familiar with identifying the elements. Also, note any questions you have about how the elements apply.)

3.2 Go around the circle again. This time take a question from the field itself. Again choose one that you feel comfortable with, don't choose one that requires you to stretch too much in your thinking. The goal here is to become comfortable thinking with the elements. (After you are finished, again note any questions that arise in you about how the elements apply. Compare the questions with the ones you identified in Exercise 3.1.) Try to pinpoint areas where the elements are not clear to you.)

3.3 Go around the circle again. This time choose a problem in the way you relate to the subject matter you're studying. For example, "Why am I studying anthropology?" "How does this course in communications fit into my life?"

The following exercises deal with individual elements rather than with going around the circle as a whole, but it's important to remember that the elements do not operate in isolation. Instead, they fit together to form the logic of the problem or question. (There will be more exercises on the elements when you are ready to put them together with the standards of critical thinking, at the end of Chapters 4 and 5.)

Each question in Exercises 3.4 through 3.13 is about one element. Each contains a list of topics, situations, excerpts, or questions. Identify that element in each of the items listed. (Your instructor may have you do some of these exercises as critical discussion in groups, rather than as individual written responses. If so, he or she may ask you to write a brief report on the discussion.)

3.4 Purpose.

a. Identify the purpose of three important regular activities in your life.

b. What is the purpose of Chapter 1 in your textbook?

c. What are your instructor's goals for you in this class. Be specific.

d. Try to identify an activity in your life where you do not entirely know your purpose.

e. Pick out three activities you engage in regularly where you tend to lose sight of your purpose.

3.5 Question at Issue.

a. Identify the main problem in how you get along with someone you are close to.

b. What is the q at i in Chapter 3 of this critical thinking text?

c. What are three main problems experts are addressing in the field you are studying? (Though these may not be problems you will actually be studying, they will be problems at the cutting edge of the field.) If you don't know, describe a realistic way of finding out.

d. Here is part of a table of contents for an art book:[4]

CHAPTER 6. SPACE

GEOMETRIC PROJECTIONS 143

SCIENTIFIC PERSPECTIVE 144

ATMOSPHERIC PERSPECTIVE 156

SPACE IN FRENCH IMPRESSIONISM 160

CEZANNE'S PERSPECTIVE OF COLOR 162

THE UNCANNY SPACE OF CUBISM 164

On the basis of this very limited amount of information, try to identify three major questions at issue to be addressed in the chapter.

e. Using only the table of contents, apply Exercise 3.5d to a chapter from a subject-matter book you are using in *this* course.

3.6 Assumptions.

a. Identify assumptions you make about someone who is important in your life.

b. Identify assumptions that person makes about you (check with them afterward).

c. Identify a *theory* that is important in the field you are studying. (Describe it in a paragraph.)

   d. Identify two assumptions in this excerpt from an economics textbook:

> The concept of "needs" encourages all-or-nothing thinking. That's why economists prefer the concept of *demand*. Demand is a concept that *relates amounts people want to obtain to the sacrifices they must make to obtain these amounts.*[5]

(Try to identify assumptions here even if you know very little about economics.)

   e. Identify two assumptions from a paragraph near the beginning of your textbook.

3.7 Implications and Consequences.

   a. Identify some implications and consequences of the syllabus for your course.

   b. What are some implications and consequences of an important decision that is coming up for you?

   c. A general statement usually has different implications from a specific or personal statement. Describe the differences in the implications of the following pairs of statements:

     (i) "This course is boring" versus "I am bored by this course."

     (ii) "Your behavior is offensive" versus "Your behavior is offensive to me."

     (iii) "I hate this class" versus "I hate this class sometimes."

Which of each pair do you think the speaker has more evidence for?

   d. Here is a sentence from a geography text: "The earth varies greatly from place to place in the total amount of energy received annually from the sun and in the resulting air temperatures."[6] Use your best judgment to identify some important implications of that claim.

   e. Identify implications of three important sentences from your text.

3.8 Information.

   a. Focus on an important decision you need to make: what information do you have about it?

   b. For the same decision, what information do you need?

   c. Identify the five most important pieces of information from Chapter 2 of your text (or some other reading). Describe how that information fits together.

d. Summarize and describe the subject-matter information you will need to do well in this course.

✳ e. Describe a situation in your life where you made a bad decision because you lacked information that was readily available to you.

3.9 Concepts.

a. Focus on a relationship you have with someone, a relationship that has a specific name (e.g., sister, mother, friend, business partner, teammate). What is your concept of that relationship? (E.g., What is it to be someone's *sister?*)

b. Describe your concept of "learning the subject" in the discipline you are studying.

✳ c. Consider the concept *animal.* That seems like a straightforward concept: we all know what an animal is. But consider this:

Cockfighting is legal in Louisiana. In cockfighting, two roosters are placed in a ring. They violently peck and gouge one another until one dies. Onlookers cheer. Louisiana also has a law prohibiting cruelty to animals. To forestall a lawsuit, the Attorney General reconciled these two laws by ruling that cockfighting is permissible because roosters are not animals!

Of course that's ridiculous. Of course the Attorney General knows roosters *are* animals. What he ruled was that when lawmakers prohibited cruelty to animals, they did not intend for it to apply to roosters. So, roosters are not *legally* animals.

Your state has a law prohibiting cruelty to animals. What are some animals that you are legally allowed to kill with a painful death? So what *is* the concept of *animal*, legally, in your state?

d. Identify the three main concepts in Chapter 1 of your textbook.

3.10 Interpretations, Conclusions.

a. Identify three conclusions you have drawn about the importance of critical thinking in classes.

b. In your book, find an example of an interpretation the author is giving. Describe the information that the interpretation is based on.

c. After some careful reflection, give an example of when you have seriously misinterpreted another person's behavior. What information did you base your interpretation on? How should you have interpreted that information?

✱ A psychology experiment was performed to see when people would violate a cultural norm against littering. Robert Cialdini and his colleagues tested the conditions under which drivers would litter a parking lot:

> Specifically, when the experimenters had previously littered the parking lot with fliers, the majority of the drivers simply followed suit—probably thinking, "after all, if no one cares about the cleanliness of the parking lot, why should I?" Interestingly enough, people were much less likely to litter if there was one piece of litter on the ground nearby than if the parking lot were completely free of litter. The reason is that seeing one piece of litter reminds us of litter—and shows us that the vast majority of people are subscribing to that norm. If the parking lot is free of litter, most people probably do not even think about the norm and, therefore, will be more likely to litter mindlessly.[7]

What part of the excerpt is *information*, and what part of it is *interpretation*?

3.11 Point of View.

    a. Describe the difference between your instructor's point of view on the subject matter of this course and your point of view on it.

    b. Describe two prominent points of view within the discipline you are studying.

✱ The editors of an anthology in social ethics describe the views of Peter Singer, a famous advocate of animal rights:

> Singer rejects speciesism, which he defines as a prejudice or attitude of bias in favor of the interests of members of one's own species and against those of members of other species. In his view, speciesism is analogous to racism and sexism. Just as we have a moral obligation to give equal consideration to the interests of all human beings, regardless of sex or skin color, so, too, we have a moral obligation to give equal consideration to the interests of animals. Insofar as animals, like humans, have the capacity to suffer, they have an interest in not suffering. Not to take that interest into account is speciesist and immoral.[8]

Describe Singer's point of view in your own words (not in the editor's words).

    d. In a single paragraph, succinctly describe the point of view of the discipline you are studying.

e. Describe your point of view on the issue of regurgitation versus critical thinking in your courses.

3.12 Alternatives.

a. Identify some goal you want to achieve in relation to this class. Describe a way you can achieve that goal. Then, describe another way to achieve that goal. Then, describe yet another way.

b. Look back over the responses you've given to any of the questions before this. Pick out two that you are least satisfied with. Describe why. Revise them by writing alternative responses.

c. Focus on an important decision you have to make: what realistic choices do you have?

d. Describe how thinking in terms of alternatives is important within the discipline you are studying. Give clear examples.

e. After reflection, describe a situation in the past where you felt you had one, and only one, course of action available to you, and you took it, but where you now realize you had alternatives that would have been better. Describe the alternatives and why you could not see them at the time.

3.13 Context.

a. Describe how the field you are studying fits into the context of other closely related fields (e.g., if it is a social science, how is it similar to and different from the other social sciences?).

b. Describe the historical background of the field you are studying.

c. Identify an area or activity that is important to you, maybe the kind of music you like, the kind of sports or leisure activity you engage in, the kind of occupation you are interested in, the kind of books you read. Sketch out as well as you can when that particular area or activity was invented, discovered, or became widespread. Try to get a sense of how ancient or how recent it is.

d. Read the first chapter of your text and describe how it sets forth the context of the field you are studying.

e. Describe a situation where, because of your personal history or your cultural background, you were unable to grasp something important that was going on. Then, describe a situation where your history or cultural background gave you a deeper insight into what was going on.

3.14 Spend a day on an element. Keep a log.

Pick one of the elements. For example, if you choose assumptions, spend your day looking for assumptions. Write down any of them you can find. Note whether they were assumptions that were clear in the person's mind or ones that the person was unaware of. Look for assumptions underlying your own statements and those of other people, in the way appliances work (or don't work), in advertising, in classes, everywhere. Feel free to ask people: "Excuse me, but I'm doing a critical thinking assignment. I just heard you speaking. Are you making the assumption that _____?"

In your log, write down any questions that come up for you about assumptions. Those may be questions you'll want to ask in class, of your teacher, or of a classmate.

Wait a few days. Then choose another element to spend a day on. Go through all of them, including context and alternatives. By the time you have finished, you should be significantly better at identifying the elements and using them in practice.

Group work

3.15 **Answer with an element.** Sit in groups of four people, A, B, C, and D. Everyone takes turns asking questions of A. They can be any question, but try to ask different kinds. Before actually answering the question, A identifies the *element* he or she is using. Afterward, switch roles: everyone quizzes B, then C, then D. For example:

Question: What's your name?

A: A piece of information. My name is A.

Question: Where do you live?

A: Another piece of information (it's getting boring). My address is . . .

Question: Why are you taking this class?

A: My major purpose is . . .

Question: What is this stupid exercise for?

A: The question at issue, from your point of view, is "What is this stupid exercise for?"

3.16 **Critical metacognitive discussion.** Choose one element per class. Discuss how that element is important in the discipline. Do some pre-thinking and pre-writing the night before as homework. Have concrete examples of that element to share.

Chapter 4

Standards of Critical Thinking

T wo primary ingredients turn thinking into critical thinking. The first is that critical thinking is *reflective* thinking. It involves a degree of thinking *about* one's thinking, specifically about the *elements* of the thinking. The second is that critical thinking is thinking that is done *well*. It is thinking that meets high *standards* of thinking.

This chapter focuses on seven of the standards our thinking has to meet for it to be critical:

- clearness
- accuracy
- importance, relevance
- sufficiency

- depth
- breadth
- precision

FIGURE 4.1 *The standards of reasoning.*

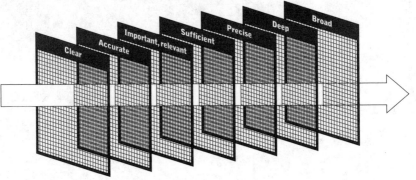

You can picture the standards as a set of screens or filters that screen out reasoning that is not clear, not accurate, or not sufficiently relevant, deep, broad, or precise. An overall Standards Check appears on pp. 144–145 at the end of this chapter.

Clearness

- Is the thinking clear?

- Is this clear in my mind?

- Am I saying this clearly?

DEFINITION: Your thinking is clear when it's easily understood, when it's free from the likelihood of misunderstanding, when it's readily apparent what follows from it.

RELATED TERMS: understandable, plain.

OPPOSITES: Your thinking is *unclear* when it is obscure, ambiguous, confused, easily misunderstood, or you don't see what follows from it.

Discussion

Expressing Yourself Clearly and Thinking Clearly in Your Own Mind

There are two aspects to clearness. One is being clear in your own mind about what you mean; the other is expressing yourself clearly so that the other person knows what you mean. Clearness as a criti-

Clearness and concepts. The following is a good way to grasp the element *concepts* better, and a way to grasp the standard *clearness* better also.

- Take a concept like "terrorist" and try to get clear about it by asking yourself about the *implications* of being a terrorist:

  - What would someone who is a terrorist do?

  - What would a terrorist refrain from doing?

  - Is there anything you can think of that people who are terrorists would *have to* do (if they didn't, they wouldn't be terrorists)?

- What are the links between terrorism and other related terms, such as violence, freedom fighter, innocent victims, and political motives?

Answering questions like these helps you to focus on the concept *terrorism*.

Apply these questions to the f&p concepts in your course.

cal thinking standard is based on a metaphor, as when we say that water is clear, or something is clear as glass. "Clear" in these cases means we can see through to the other side without anything getting in the way. In a clear picture or a clear diagram, we can readily make out what is going on. Similarly, you express yourself clearly when someone can see through your words directly to what you intended. Your thinking is clear in your own mind when you can see through to the implications of what you're thinking.

UNCLEAR EXPRESSION. There is an old joke about a father asking questions of his 12-year-old son:

"Where did you go?"

"Out."

"What did you do?"

"Nothing."

That's unclear *expression*. The boy knows exactly where he went and what he did. He's just not telling.

UNCLEAR IN MIND. You may not know what Kant means by "the transcendental unity of apperception." *Obviously* you don't if you haven't read Kant. But Kant is a tough philosopher to understand. Even if you have read it, have studied it *hard*, you may still not be very clear about it. You'll have only a vague, hazy understanding. You can't say it in your own words, you can't elaborate on it. It's unclear in your own mind.

This can happen with familiar concepts also. All of the following concepts have a great deal of unclearness in them: freedom, patriotism, love, religion, philosophy, courage, wisdom. Even in your own mind, you are probably not very clear about what they mean. If any of these concepts are important to you, it's worth the work to become clearer about them.

Most of the f&p concepts in your course are probably closer to these than to "the transcendental unity of apperception." F&p concepts may be more or less familiar to you, but they are probably still not concepts whose full implications you know.

Clearness Is Context Dependent

What is clear in one context is not necessarily clear in another. Here are three important contexts where you may have to adjust your standard of clearness.

AUDIENCE. To express yourself clearly, you need a clear idea of who your audience is. You must then choose your words appropriately. When explaining to a child what photosynthesis is, you'll use one set of words. When talking to a biologist, you will use a different set.

DISCIPLINE OR SUBJECT MATTER. Different disciplines use the standard of clearness in different ways. What it is to be clear in describing

One way students often fail to write clearly is by writing answers (in papers or essay exams) *for the teacher*—who already knows the material.

Take an important section of your text and explain in writing what it is saying. Write it as though you were explaining it to your teacher. Now, write it as though you were explaining it to a potential employer who does not know much about this subject. Your goal is to show the employer that you *understand* what you are talking about.

The two may be startlingly different.

the orbits of the planets may well be different from what it is to be clear when distinguishing the Renaissance from the baroque period, or doing a sociological study of life in a Swiss village.

STAGE OF THINKING. If you are thinking critically, your understanding of important concepts becomes clearer over time. For example, how clear an f&p concept is to you at the beginning of a course will be different from how clear it is to you at the end. As you progress in a course in art history, your concept of *renaissance* and *baroque* should become clearer. It is sometimes important not to strive for too much clarity right at the beginning, instead allowing time for ideas to clarify themselves. For example, you may need to let your idea for a term paper mature.

Impediments: What's Difficult About Being Clear

- saying what I mean
- being clear in my own mind
- anticipating what others will not understand
- overcoming certain emotional, physical, and mental states that inhibit clearness. Depression, for example, influences us to believe some very unclear (and also inaccurate) generalizations. We look around and feel, "Everything is hopeless." "My life is meaningless." Depression thrives on unclearness.

How to Become Clearer

Alone

- Practice trying to refine both your thoughts and what you say. Remind yourself to be careful to choose the clearest words.
- Anticipate places where others may have difficulty following you.
- Keep in mind who your audience is.
- Restate what you mean in other words.
- Write down your thinking. Come back to it in a few days (when it is no longer so fresh in your mind what you meant) and see what it conveys to you.
- Give examples. Also, give *contrasting* examples: examples of what you *don't* mean. (If you are talking about X, clarify it by giving examples of X and also of not-X.)
- Try out hypothetical cases.
- Extrapolate to new cases.

With Others

- Get feedback from others about what they understand you to mean.
- Ask others for examples, extrapolations, and hypothetical cases to see if you are being understood.
- Ask others in a group to paraphrase what you said or wrote. If they are easily able to paraphrase it, that is pretty solid evidence that you were clear. If they are not easily able to say what you meant, that is *some* evidence that you were unclear. (It is not strong evidence, however, because *they* may not be reading or listening attentively.)
- Get feedback from people outside your group and from those who don't look at the issue the same way you do. (Shared background makes it easier to take it for granted that people will understand you.)

Accuracy

- Is the thinking accurate?
- Are the statements accurate, true?

DEFINITION: Aristotle gave one of the clearest definitions of the term *true*:

> To say of what is that it is, or of what is not that it is not, is true.

We could define *accuracy* in much the same way:

> My thinking and my words are accurate when they describe the way things actually are.

RELATED TERMS: true, well-established, confirmed, corroborated, well-authenticated, plausible.

OPPOSITES: My thinking and my words are *inaccurate* when they are not in accord with the way things in fact are. Notice that my words can be inaccurate or false even if I *believe* they are in accord with reality. What matters for accuracy is not whether I believe something, but whether that something actually fits the way things in fact are.

Discussion

Philosophical issues about accuracy and truth arise for some people.

PROBLEMS WITH THE TERM *TRUE*. Many people reserve the word "true" for situations where they are *absolutely* sure of something, or they reserve it for profound statements ("We hold these truths to be self-evident"). It is important to notice that the word *true* as a standard of critical thinking is *not* used in either of those two ways. As a standard, it means simply that your words describe the way things are. (For example, it's true that snow is usually white, that $7 + 5 = 12$, that objects fall toward the earth at 32 ft/sec^2.) A good deal of the information we all have is likely to be true (though of course not all of it is). The information we find in reputable textbooks and course work, where authors have worked at presenting the most reliable, well-established findings and conclusions, is more likely to be true (though, again, not all of it is). But, if philosophical problems about the word "true" interfere with your critical thinking, use the term "accurate" instead.

ACCURATE VERSUS "HOW DO WE KNOW IT'S ACCURATE?" To say something is true or accurate is not always the same as saying we *know* it's true or accurate. Take the idea of life on other planets in the universe: Either there is or there isn't. We don't know which. We may never know. Yet, it should be clear that—independent of whether we ever know it—one side or the other is true.

ACCURACY AND MAKING MISTAKES. You need to be reasonable. You need to judge accuracy and truth by doing the best you can, using your best reasoning and the most reliable sources. You may turn out to be mistaken, of course. But it's not critical thinking to hold yourself or others to unreasonably high standards. The fact that it is *possible* that you made mistakes does not show that your reasoning is not accurate. Only one thing shows that your most informed and reasoned conclusions are inaccurate: *better reasoned and informed* conclusions.

Group work. Individually write down a list of statements that, by your best overall judgment and knowledge, are accurate. Try to include statements from many different domains (personal life, course work, jobs). Include some statements you would classify as hard facts, but also include some statements that, though not hard facts, seem to you, based on the best available evidence, to be true. Also include some statements containing qualifier words like *often* or *most*: those statements can be accurate too.

Discuss in groups of three or four. See if you can come to consensus as to the statements' accuracy.

Impediments: What's Difficult about Being Accurate and Recognizing What's Accurate

- It is often hard to be open to the accuracy of things we hear, especially if what we hear is threatening to us.
- Inertia. It is more comfortable to keep the beliefs we have than to change them, even when we get evidence that our beliefs are not accurate.
- Wishful thinking and denial. We often let our desires or our fears influence our assessments of what's accurate. The desire to win the lottery blinds us to the fact that we have no realistic chance to win it. People often blind themselves to their own alcoholism and the alcoholism of those they are closest to.
- We often generalize too quickly, especially from vivid personal experience. This makes us less than open to findings that contradict our personal experience. (If I visit Chicago, all it takes is a few rude Chicagoans for me to conclude that Chicagoans are rude—even though I was mistreated by only three people, and there are three *million* other Chicagoans out there.)

  A good informal way to test the accuracy of a generalization is not to look primarily for corroborating examples, but to look for counterexamples. If I believe that Chicagoans are rude, instead of looking for rude Chicagoans to confirm my generalization, I should look for Chicagoans who are *not* rude. Finding only a few reduces the credibility of my generalization. A good way to test for accuracy is to search hard for *dis*confirmation.
- We often believe folk wisdom over well-corroborated findings. (Some herbal remedies can be beneficial: but the way to tell is to check on which have been found to be beneficial under controlled tests.)

Evaluate the *accuracy* of the Golden Rule: "Do unto others as you would have them do unto you."

You can probably think of a hundred examples in favor of this generalization. But that doesn't show that the generalization is accurate pure and simple.

Think of a good counterexample: a case where it would be wrong for a person to do something unto others, even if the person would want others to do the same thing unto him or her.[1]

■ We often draw conclusions about what the world is like from news reports that tend to report on what is *unusual* or newsworthy rather than consulting informational reports such as almanacs, readily available Census Bureau data, the *Statistical Abstracts of the United States*, or textbooks. In contrast to the news, sources like these focus on what *usually* happens, and give a far more accurate picture of what our world is like.

How to Become More Accurate

Alone

■ Check out questionable information.

■ Consult reliable sources.

■ Test beliefs you hold. Treat them as *hypotheses*.

■ Be on the lookout for wishful thinking.

■ Get in the habit of reflecting on what you believe, read, and hear by asking questions that probe for accuracy:

  ■ Where did I learn that?

  ■ How reliable was my source in this context?

  ■ How could I check it?

  ■ How could I test it?

  ■ Can I think of counterexamples?

With Others

■ Get feedback on what aspects of your thinking others consider doubtful or questionable.

■ Get feedback on where they believe you need more reasons for what you say.

Importance, Relevance

■ Does the thinking focus on what is important?

■ How relevant, central, important is the thinking for the problem at hand?

DEFINITION: To say something is important is to say that it *matters*. If you're thinking about an issue, the thinking is important when it matters in deciding that issue. The thinking is important when it's directly relevant to addressing the problem at hand.

RELATED TERMS: relevant, main, central, essential, significant, crucial, critical.

OPPOSITES: You are focusing on what is unimportant if it makes no difference in relation to the question you're addressing. Your thinking can focus on a minor aspect of the problem. At an extreme, your thinking can be irrelevant to the problem at hand.

Discussion

IMPORTANT *TO*, RELEVANT *TO*. In critical thinking, *relevant* means relevant *to* a question at issue, with a purpose in mind and set in a particular context. It doesn't mean relevant in general. The same is true for the term *important*.

Everything is relevant to *something*, but that does not mean it's relevant to the problem at hand. When we evaluate a piece of reasoning, what we are interested in is whether that reasoning is relevant or important to deciding the question at issue.

IMPORTANT TO YOU VERSUS IMPORTANT FOR REASONING THROUGH THE QUESTION AT ISSUE. There are many things that are vitally important to me personally: my health, for example, or the well-being of my family, or the emotions I am feeling. It can feel insulting for someone to tell me that such considerations are not relevant, or not important. Yet, those considerations can indeed be irrelevant to reasoning through a particular question at issue.

For example, victims of violent crime often have intense feelings of anger and outrage. However, those feelings are not relevant to the question of whether the person accused is guilty or innocent. In fact, the intensity of those feelings can even make the question of guilt harder to decide reasonably. Obviously, victims' feelings of anger and violation *are* important—important to *them* and important to *us* as empathetic fellow humans. But the feelings are *not* important when deciding whether someone is guilty. Only the evidence of the case (motivation, identification by witnesses, circumstantial evidence, etc.) is relevant to arriving at a just verdict.

Impediments: What's Difficult about Focusing on What Is Important

- losing sight of your purpose in reasoning the question out
- forgetting or ignoring the context of the question
- missing the forest for the trees

- thinking that everything in a course or subject matter is equally important
- speaking just to be speaking; writing just to be filling pages
- responding without reflecting
- having an agenda that gets in the way of what you hear and read
- being threatened or preoccupied, or making reactions seem relevant to the problem at hand, even when they aren't.

How to Focus on What Is Most Important

Alone

- Remind yourself to keep in mind the question at issue, your purpose, and the context in which the question is being asked.
- Take a step back in your thinking: try to get an overview.
- Ask: How does this point relate to the topic at hand?
- *Outline.* Outline what you read or hear. Outline your own thoughts on a question. In your outline, distinguish between main points and subsidiary points.
- *Summarize.* Write a *short* summary of what you read or hear. (Then maybe make it shorter still.)
- Sketch a quick concept map. (See pp. 63–65)
- When listening or reading, focus on what is being said and put aside your *reaction* to what is said.

With Others

- Compare your outlines and summaries with those of other people in a group. Exchange honest but respectful feedback on what is relevant to a question and what is not.
- Practice picking out what is essential *to the other person.* Ask: "Is this the central part of what you are saying?"

Sufficiency

- Has this been reasoned out sufficiently?

- Have I reasoned this out enough to decide the issue reasonably?

DEFINITION: Your thinking about a question or issue is *sufficient* when you've reasoned it out thoroughly enough for the purpose at hand, when it is adequate for what is needed, when you've taken account of all necessary factors.

RELATED TERMS: adequate, enough, complete, comprehensive, thorough.

OPPOSITES: Your thinking is *insufficient* when you have left out crucial considerations, when you haven't reasoned the issue out enough to meet the needs of the situation, when there are other essential factors for you to address before you decide this issue.

Discussion

SUFFICIENCY, PURPOSE, AND CONTEXT. A basic question is always: "Have I reasoned this out enough?" A follow-up question is always: "Enough for *what?*" A reasonable answer to the second question is: "Enough to achieve the purpose." It is also reasonable to add: "Enough to achieve it in this particular setting or context."

One crucial context is the **time factor.** I may have to make a decision about a patient whose life is in immediate danger. How much reasoning is sufficient under those circumstances depends heavily on the fact that it's an *emergency.* An administrator, reviewing the decision later, has much more time to evaluate what should have been done.

SUFFICIENCY, ACCURACY, AND RELEVANCE. As standards, accuracy and relevance are much more familiar to the general population than sufficiency. It's not enough, however, for someone's reasons to be *accurate* and *relevant.* The reasons also have to be *enough* to draw the conclusion. For example, it is *true* that the Constitution guarantees the right to bear arms, and this is certainly *relevant* to handgun legislation, but it's not *sufficient* to show that handguns should be legal. There are at least four or five other main issues that need to be adequately reasoned through before this conclusion could be reached.

SUFFICIENCY VERSUS PROOF. It is always a temptation to say that you need more information before deciding this issue, but it's unreasonable to require too *much* evidence before drawing a conclusion. Usually, important, practical issues cannot be proved conclusively. No one can *prove* what is the best overall procedure for teaching math in an elementary education classroom because there are many reasonable alternatives. We usually cannot have complete evidence that an action will be environmentally safe; all we can have is strong evidence, and even that is usually hard to come by. Scientists usually maintain that scientific laws are not *proven* by experiments—rather, they are *confirmed* by experiment, always allowing for the fact that some later experiments may disconfirm the law, especially in the light of a new scientific theory.

So requiring enough reasoning to *prove* a case *conclusively* will usually be an unreasonably stringent standard.

A COURTROOM ANALOGY. How much reasoning is enough? In criminal cases, guilt has to be established beyond a reasonable doubt. That is a measure of how *sufficient* the evidence in the case has to be. The standard is set very high because a person's freedom depends on the outcome.

In civil cases like lawsuits, on the other hand, all that is required is a preponderance of evidence. The judge or jury merely has to decide which of the two sides has more evidence in its favor.

SUFFICIENCY AND DEDUCTIVE VALIDITY. The term *validity*—often called *deductive validity*—is used in formal logic. Deductive validity is actually a more stringent concept than proof as used in a courtroom. For an argument to be deductively valid, the premises (if true) have to prove the conclusion not just beyond any *reasonable* doubt, but beyond any *possible* doubt as well. A familiar example is the syllogism:

Socrates is human.

All humans are mortal.

Therefore, Socrates is mortal.

This is an important concept for those dealing with formal logic or the foundations of mathematics.

SUFFICIENCY AND SUCCESS. Suppose you reason out an important decision (like the one in the box to the right), and you do so to the best of your ability under the circumstances. Suppose that, nevertheless, the decision turns out disastrously. Did you reason it out sufficiently? Well, if you did reason it out to the best of your ability under the circumstances, the answer is yes.

The *success* of a decision can never be the measure of whether you've reasoned something out enough. Success depends on many other factors besides good reasoning, and many of those factors are beyond

> After reasoning through the decision, parents let their sixteen-year-old son, a new driver, take the car out. There is an accident. The son is seriously hurt. The parents feel intensely guilty. "If only we hadn't let him take the car out. . . . We should not have made that decision."

your control, and beyond your ability to anticipate. A successful decision depends, for example, on luck, the right (or the wrong) combination of events occurring at just the right moment in time.

Many times our *feelings* respond as if we had not done enough, as in the case of the parents letting the son drive. That's because *grief* often presents itself to us as *guilt*. Feelings like guilt and shame are not a good guide to whether we have reasoned decisions out sufficiently. It is more reasonable to let the grief come out purely as grief, mourning our loss but without self-recrimination.

Impediments: What's Difficult about Reasoning Through Something Sufficiently

- jumping to conclusions
- a tendency to reason through unimportant issues too much and through important issues too little
- sticking with pre-established views that seem sufficient because we have not examined alternatives
- unreasonable standards (such as perfectionism) of what counts as enough
- lack of relevant background knowledge
- simply forgetting to ask, "Is this sufficient?" "Is it enough?"

How to Reason Things Out Sufficiently

Alone

- Ask yourself explicitly: "Has enough evidence been given? Has enough of the purpose been accomplished? Has the question been addressed sufficiently?" Such questions can be asked for each of the elements.
- List the relevant factors that need to be decided before you can come to a reasonable conclusion about the main one.
- Consciously seek out alternatives. Ask yourself: What are the alternatives to the conclusion being drawn? How much reasoning is sufficient to decide between them?
- Take more time to reason out important issues thoroughly.
- Acquire necessary background knowledge.
- Practice. (A good source for practice: Look around for news reports about findings in the field or discipline you are studying, ones where your knowledge of the field can lead you to say

that the reported findings are not enough to draw the conclusions stated in the report.)

With Others

- Ask fellow students for alternatives they see and maybe you don't.
- *Before* you try to answer a critical thinking question, discuss with others how much evidence is necessary to answer it.
- Get feedback from experts on whether your reasoning about an issue in the field is sufficient.

In each item below, a reason is given → then a conclusion is drawn. In each case explain why the reason is *not enough* to draw the conclusion. Do not *disagree* with the reason; focus instead on why it's not *sufficient*.

1. My 80-year-old grandfather smoked a pack of cigarettes a day his whole life. → Cigarettes are not harmful.

2. I've studied every night for a week. → I'll do well on the exam.

3. You have lied to me. → Now I can never trust you.

4. "I cried because I had no shoes, until I met a man who had no feet." → I shouldn't cry about my own suffering.

5. The Bible says "Thou shalt not kill." → Capital punishment is forbidden by the Bible.

Depth and Breadth

- Has this been reasoned out deeply enough?

- Have I taken adequate account of underlying theories, explanations, and the complexities of the problem?

- Have I reasoned this out broadly enough?

- Have I taken adequate account of other related issues, other perspectives on the problem, other aspects of the context?

DEFINITION: Your thinking about a question is deep enough when (a) you recognize that, in order to accomplish your purpose, you must look below the surface of the question or issue (particularly at theories or explanations in the discipline); (b) you identify the complexities that underlie it; and (c) you take adequate account of those complexities and underlying issues in addressing the question.

Similarly, your thinking is broad enough when you (a) recognize the need to look at other aspects, other perspectives, other parallel problems, (b) identify them, and (c) take adequate account of them in reasoning through the question.

RELATED TERMS: complex, comprehensive, nuanced (sometimes), subtle (sometimes), probing, root questions.

OPPOSITES: Your thinking is *too superficial* or *too narrow* when you oversimplify things; when you don't see that complex, multifaceted issues require complex, multifaceted responses; when you act as if large-scale, controversial issues are susceptible to easy answers and quick fixes.

Discussion

DIFFERENCES BETWEEN DEPTH AND BREADTH. Depth and breadth are aspects of sufficiency: the question is always, "Is the person reasoning this out deeply *enough* (or broadly *enough*) to accomplish his or her purpose?" The two standards are not always clearly distinguishable. The goal is to develop an intuitive feel for when it is important to delve more deeply into an issue, and when it is important to look at it more broadly by taking account of other related issues.

The difference is one of emphasis, a difference of where to direct your reasoning. Imagine yourself on a path going toward a destination. Breadth says to look around you, at the forest, fields, mountains, other travelers, the impending weather. Depth asks you to look deeper: at the solidity of the path itself, the state of your muscles when walking it, the strength of your desire to reach the destination, your knowledge of the human body's need for nutrition. One directs you to look around, to take a more comprehensive view of things; the other directs you to look below the surface, to see things in all their depth.

DEPTH AND THEORY. One fruitful way to gain depth in your thinking is to look at the theoretical underpinnings of the question you are considering. Often we operate by a rule of thumb: Take daily multivitamins, discipline your children without shaming them, set performance quotas as an important part of sales management. When these situations become problematic though, a good place to

Suppose I'm a student and I'm dissatisfied with the grades I've been receiving. "I study—and still my grades are not as high as they should be." A good thing to do is to *broaden* my thinking. What are some other, more effective ways to study? Who can I consult about these? Are there other skills—reading skills, outlining skills, even shorthand skills—that will help me take better notes?

I can also look more *deeply* (this would be especially called for if I have tried other perspectives without improving the results): What underlies my difficulty in getting good grades even though I study a lot?

Psychological attitudes are a good place to look for depth. Depression, for example, often results in "shooting myself in the foot" right before exams. I may have unrealistic expectations of myself. Self-deception can also enter in: I think I'm studying a lot, but much of that time is spent worrying about studying, rather than studying. Maybe my concept of studying is off-base: I may be regurgitating information when the teacher expects me to reason things out (or vice versa). Maybe I'm not really hearing what the teacher is saying.

look is at the theory that underlies them: nutrition theory, child-development theory, and sales management theory. Theories answer, in far greater depth, the questions of *why* you should, or should not, follow the rule of thumb. One of the major payoffs of learning to think in a discipline is this ability to go deeper into the theory for greater understanding.

DEPTH: SUPERFICIAL VERSUS SURFACE. Richard Paul makes a nice distinction: my thinking is *superficial* when I take a question that requires in-depth treatment but my reasoning about it leaves out the important complexities. "Question: What can we do about the problem of violent crime in the U.S.? Answer: Tougher law enforcement. Period." The answer is superficial.

Often though, the problem we are addressing requires that we not go into depth, but focus on the *surface logic*, those specific aspects needed to solve a specific problem. "Question: Where is the restroom?" The appropriate response addresses the surface of things: "Down the hall, turn left, third door on your right." The appropriate response is not "Why?"

Here is an example of depth and theory that seems (to me) both simple and amazing.

We all know that hot air rises. That's accurate as far as it goes. But it's not *deep*. Physically, there is no *force* that makes light things rise. The deeper truth is that *cold* air *falls*. It's heavier, so gravity pulls it downward—the cold air then crowds the hot air out of the way. Hot air doesn't exactly "rise"—it's pushed upward.

So, looked at deeply, what happens when wood *floats* on water?

Impediments: What's Difficult about Reasoning Deeply Enough and Broadly Enough

- It is difficult to live with the ambiguity and uncertainty that attend reasonable thinking about so many complex problems. We would like things to be simpler, more clear-cut. All-or-nothing answers give us a feeling of control over complex problems, even when another part of our minds tells us that we have very little control over them. Even the illusion of control is sometimes comforting.

- Often you may not realize that there are complexities to an issue. In fact, one of the things we learn directly from disciplines is the amount of complexity there is to a seemingly simple issue.

- Recognizing that there are depths to a problem that confronts us, that there are other related perspectives on it, forces us to refuse to accept a slogan as a guide to action, or the unquestioned common sense viewpoint. It leads us to question the background logic we applied to such a problem before we took the course in the field.

How to Look Beneath the Surface of Things, How to Gain a Broader Perspective

Alone

- Ask: Do other reasonable people have different perspectives on this?

- Ask: Is there a theoretical structure underlying this issue that I need to consider? How can I look at it from that theoretical perspective?

- Work to understand theory.
- Ask: Are there other issues that underlie this?
- Expect complexities to arise when making important decisions or thinking through important issues. Expect there to be depths to these questions. Don't go in with the expectation that the answers will be simple.

With Others

- Take account of the differing perspectives of others.
- Discuss what other factors or perspectives you need to consider. Take people's feedback seriously.
- Talk about the relation between theory and practice.

Precision

- Is the thinking precise?

- Is the reasoning detailed enough?

DEFINITION: Your thinking is precise when you have been as specific and detailed as needed to reason through an issue.

RELATED TERMS: exact, specific, detailed, focused.

OPPOSITES: Your thinking is *imprecise* when you are inexact, when you don't give enough details to pinpoint what you are saying, when you are satisfied with speaking in generalities without getting down to the specific issues.

Discussion

PRECISION AND CLEARNESS. Precision and clearness are related, but they capture different ideas. This can be seen more easily with examples. Saying an infant is running a temperature is clear. It means that the infant's temperature is somewhere above 98.6 degrees. Saying that the infant is running a temperature of 102 degrees is both clear *and* precise. Saying "There is a great deal of violence on TV, even on children's programs" is clear (that is, we understand the claim that is being made); saying that "in 1993, U. S. network programs offered about 3 violent acts per hour during prime time, and 18 per hour during children's Saturday morning programs"[2] is both clear *and* precise. E. M. Forster once illustrated the difference between a story and a plot by saying that "The king died, and then the queen died" is a story; "The king died, then the queen died of grief" is a plot. Both statements are clear, but the second is considerably more precise.

PRECISION AND ACCURACY. There is no relationship between precision and accuracy: a lie can be entirely precise; a true statement can lack precision. Therefore, you can't infer that a statement is accurate from the fact that it is precise.

The problem is that precise statements give the *appearance* of accuracy. Sir John Mandeville is famous today as a lying author. In his book, *Travels*, he described traveling to distant lands and meeting people with dog's heads. One of the reasons he was so believed in his day is that his descriptions were so precise.

PRECISION AND PURPOSE. It is *not* precise to say that I am 5 foot 11.735 inches tall. A person's height cannot be measured to that degree of precision. It is not that we lack instruments that are sufficiently precise, it's that such a degree of precision is meaningless when applied to a person. Our heights change during moments of the day, and we are as much as an inch shorter at bedtime than in the morning; even subtly different ways of standing affect a measurement by tenths of an inch.

What is precise will always be relative both to the purpose of the reasoning and to the context.

PRECISION AND THINKING IN THE FIELD. It is difficult to think in a way that lets you see both the larger picture and also the details in that larger picture. Yet, that is exactly what is involved in thinking in a discipline.

Knowing a field or discipline is not at all like memorizing long lists of details. It is also not the same as knowing a bunch of generalities.

It's much more like an outline. You need to know the major, general headings. But under those headings you need to be able to give well-chosen details and exactly formulated points to make your reasoning precise and to the point.

Impediments: What's Difficult about Being Precise

- We often overlook the need to be precise.
- It takes work to be precise. It means getting specific enough to tell *exactly* what we are talking about. It's easy to settle for generalities.
- It is difficult to see the forest for the trees, but it is also difficult to see the trees for the forest.
- We are sometimes too rushed to take the time to make our reasoning precise.

How to Become More Precise

Alone

- Anticipate where others will need details to follow your reasoning.
- When you report what other people say, or the results of an experiment, or an office procedure, try to say it exactly.
- Look up details in the text.
- When you take detailed notes, do so in outline form.
- Keep going from the general to the specific and from the specific to the general: What is a specific instance of this generality? How does this detail fit into the whole picture?

With Others

- Get feedback on where you need to be more specific, more exact.
- Ask fellow students where they need you to supply more detail.

Understanding and Internalizing Critical-Thinking Standards

The goal is not just to understand the standards in the abstract. Rather, it's to incorporate them into your thinking and into your life. They don't work just separately, but together as well. If you think of them as linked together to form a whole, that whole constitutes a major part of what critical thinking is. To internalize the idea of critical thinking is to understand deeply how *critical* thinking is different from *thinking*. The standards together, formed into a whole, constitute a good deal of the *critical* part.

Additional Critical-Thinking Standards

There are additional critical thinking standards. Many of them overlap the standards already described, and some of them are critical-thinking standards in one context but not in another. Some of them are critical-thinking standards in a particular discipline. A list includes:

- reasonable
- logical
- rational
- consistent
- falsifiable

- testable
- well-organized
- authenticated
- effective
- factual

In addition, there are many terms that are used to describe the opposite of critical thinking. Informal logicians often teach a set of logical fallacies—these are ways people characteristically go wrong in their thinking. Fallacies are ways of thinking that seem to be good thinking, but actually are not.

Non–Critical-Thinking Standards

A good way to increase your understanding of how the standards constitute critical thinking is to contrast them with non–critical-thinking standards. Here are a few:

- fun
- exciting
- feels good
- attention-getting
- popular

- chic
- spontaneous
- advantageous
- beneficial to me

There is nothing inherently wrong with such standards. They are *not opposed* to critical thinking. They are simply non–critical-thinking standards.

You can see the uphill battle you have ahead of you if you want to think critically—so many influences in the world tend to push these non–critical-thinking standards on us. Think of *popularity*, for example. It's not that popularity is opposed to critical thinking. Something can be popular and *also* an example of careful thinking. (For instance, a few years ago healthy, comfortable walking shoes became a fad.) The problem is that popularity is emphasized so much as a standard—it is often so very important to us to do what is popular—that it effectively pushes accuracy, clearness, and depth aside as less important.

Similarly with *fun*. Even in education, there is a great emphasis on making learning fun. It is important to see that there is nothing intrinsically wrong with that; it is beneficial in many ways. Authentic learning *is* often fun; certainly it is often deeply gratifying and fulfilling to take ownership of an f&p concept in a discipline. Fun opposes critical thinking only when the assumption creeps in that learning *has to be* fun: that if it's not fun, we can't expect people to do it.

Catalogue for yourself the number of influences in society that promote non–critical-thinking standards. Many of these non–critical-thinking standards are excellent if you incorporate critical thinking into them. Without critical thinking, however, even seemingly benign standards can be dangerous.

Here is another list of non–critical-thinking standards, ones that go deeper than the previous list:

- evocative
- deeply felt, deeply moving
- moral, ethical
- held with deep conviction
- patriotic

- free
- religious, spiritual
- knowledgeable
- loving

These standards are essential parts of life. In a way, they may be more important than critical thinking itself. The trouble with saying that, though, is that *without* critical thinking standards incorporated into them, they can be demeaning, misplaced, hollow, and dangerous.

Naziism was extremely *evocative.* The Nuremberg Rally, according to nearly every observer, was *deeply moving.* Fanatics always hold their beliefs *with deep conviction*—that's why they are called fanatics. Among the things *held with deepest conviction* are prejudices. Without critical thinking, even *loving* can become caretaking and codependence.

Even a standard like "moral" exhibits this same two-edged quality. To be moral without focusing on accuracy, clarity, importance, without focusing on purpose, consequences, or assumptions, is virtually a contradiction. Indeed, there is a "strong sense" of critical thinking in which fairmindedness plays a defining role.[3] If you try to be moral without thinking critically, you become merely a rule-follower, not

Choose four of the non–critical-thinking standards listed above, and describe how critical thinking is necessary to the application of each standard. As part of your answer, give a *contrasting* example: describe how, without critical thinking, each of the non–critical-thinking standards is open to distortion and misguided application.

Can you think of examples from history (or from your background knowledge) where people had a deeply misguided sense of what it meant to be patriotic or religious or knowledgeable or free?

using your critical thinking skills even to assess whose rules you should follow. That is not really being moral at all.

To be moral or ethical as a person in business, a health practitioner, or any kind of professional at all *is* to think critically. It requires you to do more, for example, than merely follow the ethical codes of conduct as laid down by that profession. It requires you to identify carefully the consequences of your actions and those of the group you're a part of, to be clear about your goals, to weigh the costs and benefits of alternative courses of action (to others as well as to your group), to make hard choices about what constitutes ethical behavior based on accurate information and reasonable assumptions.

Evaluating Around the Circle

To evaluate a piece of reasoning is to make judgments about how reasonable it is; it is to assess how well it lives up to critical thinking standards.

- Going around the circle answers the question: *How* has this person thought this out?

- Evaluating around the circle answers the question: *How well* has this person thought this out?

The Basic Process of Evaluating a Piece of Reasoning

Even more than with the questions on *understanding* someone's reasoning, the following questions are *guides* only. You will have to be flexible and adapt the questions to fit the piece of reasoning you are trying to evaluate. (For example, you may need to consult the list of standards frequently. When the guideline question uses a word like "adequate" or "better," it often helps to use a more precise word from the list of standards: "Is it adequate?" can mean "Is it adequate with respect to a specific standard?" For example, "Is it deep enough?" "Is it broad enough?" "Is it complete enough, or does it omit something essential?") You also need to support the major judgments you make by giving *reasons* and *explanations*.

EVALUATING AROUND THE CIRCLE:

1. Does the person achieve his or her purpose in this piece of reasoning?
2. Does the person adequately answer the question at issue?
3. Look at the major pieces of information the person provides. Are they reasonable? Well-established? Are they on the whole true? Is more information needed to resolve the question at issue?
4. Do the person's conclusions follow from his or her reasoning? Is the person interpreting the issue accurately?
5. Are there other valid ways of understanding the central concepts, ways that would influence the outcome of the reasoning?
6. Are the person's major assumptions reasonable enough for you to agree with them?

7. Are the implications of the person's reasoning acceptable? Will the person's reasoning lead to other consequences, ones that would count for or against his or her reasoning?

8. Is the person aware of other reasonable points of view on this issue? Has he or she taken them adequately into account?

9. Does the person reason through the issue in a way that takes sufficient account of the context?

10. Are there better alternatives to the way the person has reasoned this out?

Your answers to these 10 questions can form the evaluation itself. On the other hand, it is usually beneficial to pull the various answers together. To do this, think of your answers to these 10 questions as the groundwork of your evaluation.

Now, write out (in normal paragraphs) an overall evaluation of the piece of reasoning as a whole.

a. This should be based on the most important threads from your answers to the 10 questions.

b. It should identify both the strong and the weak points of the piece of reasoning.

c. It should incorporate a standards check. (See pp. 144–145.)

d. Claims you make in your evaluation should be backed up with reasons.

A Note on Reading as a Critical-Thinking Process

In the deepest sense, reading *is* a critical thinking process, and you can become an excellent critical reader by focusing on the elements and the standards as the heart of your reading.

Critical Reading

The foundation of critical reading is reasonable, reflective *analysis* and *synthesis*. That means learning to go around the circle as you read, so that you grasp the logic of the piece and check your reading with the standards. At first, of course, this may be slow going, and a lot of the analysis and synthesis will take place after you are "finished" with the reading. You will ask yourself, reflectively, about the writer's purpose, the question at issue being addressed, the information being given—on through all the elements.

As you become proficient at critical reading, you will find that you are answering these questions *as you read*. This is critical reading in a highly integrated sense. You will be noting the author's main assumptions, conclusions, concepts, and point of view as you encounter them and as they develop, and you will be fitting them together. Even when you achieve that level of ability though, the reflection afterward remains an important part of reading. Often reading in the fullest sense—reading with understanding and appreciation—gets completed only after you put the book down, sometimes long after. After you have read some of George Eliot, Richard Dawkins, or Friedrich Nietzsche, or a biography of Mohandas Gandhi, the meanings can still continue to connect inside of you.

In addition to analyzing and synthesizing, you will also be reading *evaluatively*. That is, you will apply the standards of critical thinking not just to your understanding of the writing, but to the writing itself. You will note where writers are, in your best judgment, *accurate* or inaccurate (or somewhere in between), where they are on target (the standard of *importance*), whether they present a *sufficient* case or go *deep* enough.

As with all critical thinking, it is important to realize that these are not new processes you are being asked to do. The difference between critical reading and uncritical reading will not be *whether* you analyze, synthesize, and evaluate. It will be the degree to which you are *aware of* these processes as you engage in them (*reflective* thinking) and the degree to which you are making sound judgments about accuracy, importance, sufficiency, and the other standards (*reasonable* thinking).

Reading and the Standard of Importance

As you read, you will be focusing on the elements in a continuous way, but you will be using the standard of *importance* as a kind of filter. That is, you will focus on the elements only as the answers are important. Thus, there is little point to writing down *all* the assumptions or implications or pieces of information contained in your reading—you need to note only the important ones.

Important for what? As always, important means important for some specific purpose or question at issue. There are two major ways you can read with the standard of importance acting as your filter. First, you may want to get a full understanding of what an author is saying. In that case, you will read with an eye to seeing everything that is important for the *author's* purpose or question at issue. The second way to read is with an eye to achieving *your own* purpose or answering your own question at issue, without regard for the author's purpose or q at i. That is what happens when you skim, run through a chapter noting bold-faced terms, or use the index to locate a particular topic you are interested in.

Reading for Information

You have to be wary of the idea of reading for information. As a critical thinker, you should always read for information *plus* concepts to organize that information *plus* the logical connections between those concepts.

Reading for Pleasure

There is no opposition between reading critically and reading for pleasure, though it often seems as if there is. Sometimes people love a poem or a piece of music. They are then assigned to analyze it, and that seems to eliminate the feeling response. Sometimes people say that, after analysis, they no longer like the piece.

That is a genuine experience many people have, but it seems to come more from the spirit in which you analyze things than from the analysis itself. Sometimes when you analyze a poem, it feels as if you are dissecting it, leaving it lifeless afterward.

By way of comparison, think about your friends. If you love your friends, you may want to understand them, maybe understand them deeply. That is not the same as dissecting their personalities. Instead, you think about what their goals are, what beliefs are important to them, what the circumstances of their life are. That is an analysis—specifically, looking at purpose, assumptions, context—and it is a natural part of caring for someone. If someone is *not* interested in these, it's hard to believe that he or she really cares about you. "Analyzing" your friend can sound harsh, but it is really understanding that you are after. The same is true of studying a poem or a piece of music.

Reading and Listening

Virtually every remark about reading applies to *listening* as well. Critical listening is understanding what the speaker is saying in terms of the elements, understanding the logic of it (synthesis), and assessing your understanding of what the person is saying in terms of the standards. As with reading, much of the listening with understanding can take place after the speaker is finished. You can continue to hear the words in your head and to understand them more fully (through understanding the speaker's purpose, the conclusions being drawn, the main concepts, and so on). As your critical skills develop around the elements, a lot of your understanding will take place *as* you listen. As you practice critical listening in class, focusing on what is *important* and on *the logic of* what you are hearing, you will notice that your note-taking will change.

Students: Photocopy these pages. Check (✓) each relevant box.

CLEAR

Is **my reasoning** clear?

Do I understand this clearly?

❏ Do I know the implications?

Have I given enough

   ❏ examples?

   ❏ contrasting examples?

   ❏ hypothetical cases?

   ❏ analogies?

❏ Have I elaborated enough?

Is **my presentation** of my reasoning clear?

❏ Have I said clearly what I meant?

ACCURATE

Is **my reasoning** accurate?

Is this in accord with

   ❏ the best knowledge I have?

   ❏ the findings of the discipline?

   ❏ reliable sources?

❏ Do I need to check this out?

Check: Could this be based on

   ❏ wishful thinking?

   ❏ unexamined background stories?

   ❏ hearsay, questionable sources?

Does **my presentation** display accuracy?

Have I supported the accuracy of my claims

   ❏ with reasons?

   ❏ with *good* reasons?

IMPORTANT, RELEVANT

In **my reasoning,** have I focused on what is most important, given

   ❏ my purpose?

   ❏ the question at issue?

   ❏ the context?

- ❏ Do I have an overview?
- ❏ Can I *outline* my reasoning?
- ❏ Can I *summarize* my reasoning?
- ❏ Have I **presented** my reasoning in a way that displays what is important?

SUFFICIENT

Have I **reasoned** this through enough, given
- ❏ my purpose?
- ❏ the q at i?
- ❏ the context?
- ❏ Have I left out crucial steps?
- ❏ Have I jumped to conclusions?
- ❏ Are there other essential issues to consider?

In **my presentation**
- ❏ Have I said enough to show my audience that it is reasonable to come to my conclusions?

DEEP AND BROAD

In **my reasoning,** have I looked beneath the surface?
- ❏ at underlying explanations, theories?
- ❏ at complexities of the issue?
- ❏ Have I taken account of other relevant perspectives?

In **my presentation,** have I presented my reasoning in a way that *displays* its
- ❏ depth?
- ❏ breadth?

PRECISE

Is **my reasoning** precise enough, specific enough?
- ❏ Do I need more details?
- ❏ Do I need more exactness?
- ❏ Have I **stated** the details and degree of exactness my audience needs?

REASONABLE OVERALL

- ❏ Is my reasoning reasonable overall?
- ❏ Have I presented a reasonable overall case?

4.1 In the Chapter 3 exercises, you went around the circle with respect to three different questions. Complete a standards check (pp. 144–145) for each of your responses, correcting and filling in aspects of your response where needed.

4.2 **Working in pairs on the standards.** Choose some piece of writing you have done in the course (at least two or three paragraphs, preferably involving critical thinking in the discipline). Duplicate it before you come to class, and exchange copies with your partner.

The exercise is to give your partner useful feedback on one of the standards, in this case, clearness. Turn to the section "How to Become Clearer . . . With Others" (p. 122). Using those questions as a guide, give your partner feedback on what he or she has written.

4.3 You can do Exercise 4.2 in seven different installments, one on each of the standards. It can be done over half a semester or over the whole semester, a little bit at a time. Choose different pieces of writing each time.

4.4 Here is a paragraph from a geography text:

> Culture, many argue, is the adhesive binding together of the world's diverse social fabric. A cursory read of the daily newspaper, however, raises questions as to whether the world is literally coming unglued since the frequency and the intensity of cultural conflict seems pervasive and ever-increasing. With the recent rise of global communication systems (satellite TV, movies, video, etc.) stereotypic Western culture is spreading at a rapid pace. While this is willingly accepted by many throughout the world, other groups and countries resist this new form of cultural imperialism through protests, censorship, and restrictions on film, TV, and music.[5]

Identify the elements of reasoning as they occur in the paragraph. Next, evaluate the paragraph using the standards of critical thinking.

4.5 As in Exercise 4.4, engage in the same kind of evaluative reflection with respect to important readings in your text in the discipline. Focus on key paragraphs, chapter summaries and reviews, case studies, entire books. Identify the elements in the readings. Next, evaluate the readings using the standards. (You evaluate, remember, not just for accuracy, but for how clear the reading is to you, whether it has been explained sufficiently for you to follow it, whether you can see its importance in the whole, etc.)

4.6 **Spend a day on a standard. Keep a log.** Pick one of the standards. Let's say you've chosen clearness. Spend your day looking for instances of clearness and unclearness, writing down any of them you can find. Note if examples would have helped, if more elaboration was needed, if the speaker lost sight of the intended audience. Write down examples you find of things that were probably unclear in the person's mind. Also write down examples of things that may have been clear in the person's mind, but were not stated or written clearly. Find examples in your own statements and in those of other people, on TV, in conversations with friends, lectures in classes, anywhere. In your log, write down any questions that come up for you. Those may be questions you'll want to ask in class, of your teacher, or of a critical-thinking classmate.

Wait a few days. Then choose another standard to spend a day on. Go through all seven. By the time you have finished, you should find that you both understand and can apply the standards significantly better than before.

4.7 As you read your text, pick out the five most important points in a chapter. Read about them the way you would normally. Then, close your book. Restate each of those claims in your own words. Evaluate your restatement on the basis of *clearness.* Give examples of your own. Elaborate as needed. Afterward, work in a group to get feedback from others.

4.8 Repeat Exercise 4.7 when you read the next chapter, but this time use a standard other than clearness.

4.9 Referring back to the discussion in Chapter 3, evaluate Chris's reasoning about marriage by evaluating around the circle (pp. 140–141). Is it biased against gays to use the concept of marriage as a major example? When you read the example, which gender, if any, did you assume Chris and Sean each were?

The next three questions are related to one another.

4.10 Take each important piece of reading you are required to do in the course and engage in critical reading by going around the circle.

4.11 When you finish Exercise 4.10, do a standards check on your reasoning.

4.12 Still using the material from exercise 4.10, evaluate the reasoning in the piece itself: *How well* has the writer reasoned out the issue? Do this by evaluating around the circle.

4.13 **Ask with a standard.** Sit in groups of four. At any one point in the discussion, one person (A) will be answering questions, and three people (B, C, and D) will be asking questions regarding a standard:

B asks A a question. (For example, "Why are you taking this course?")

A answers. (For example, "It's a requirement for my major.")

From then on, B, C, and D ask A questions, each time in reference to a standard. (For example, "Can you make that clearer?" "Is that the most important reason?" "Do you have other important reasons?" "Can you take a broader perspective?")

A keeps answering. (The questions have to make sense given A's responses.)

Then switch roles, with everyone asking questions-with-a-standard of B, then C, then D.

4.14 Do at least a quick standards check for every piece of written work you do in this course.

4.15 **Group work.**   Separate into seven groups in the class. Each group will serve as the authority for one of the standards. Prepare a presentation on the standard. Equitably decide who will perform each part of the presentation:

- Explain what the standard is.
- Give good examples of its use in the discipline.
- Give contrasting examples.
- Tell what the implications and consequences are when reasoning does not meet the standard.

Chapter 5

Putting It All Together: Answering Critical-Thinking Questions

I t would be natural at this point if you felt a large number of fragments swirling around in your head. First, there are the 8+ elements. Then, there are the standards, seven of them discussed in some detail. At this point, you probably have a mixed grasp of the elements, the standards, and critical thinking as a whole.

You are probably good at identifying some of the elements when you read a chapter or think through a problem on your own, and you are not nearly as good at identifying some of the other elements. You may be strong on identifying an author's purpose or the information an author is providing, but you may not be clear about the exact difference between conclusions and implications, and you may have trouble telling an assumption from a concept.

The same is probably true of your grasp of the standards. You may find that you are regularly giving examples to make your thinking clearer. But it may be difficult to tell when you have reasoned through a question sufficiently.

These all improve with practice and instruction—frequently checking back with the book, doing the exercises, or receiving feedback from your teacher. You may still be concerned that you don't see clearly how this all fits together. You may wonder, "Where am I in the process? How do I get an overview?" "I need some kind of a map, so I know which way to go, which critical-thinking move to make, and why." If you feel that way, it's based on a sound instinct. Part of understanding anything, critical thinking included, is seeing *the whole* and *the parts* in perspective: seeing how it all fits together. The purpose of this chapter is to give a sense of the whole, to provide a map.

The Core Process of Critical Thinking

So, what do critical thinkers do?

Core Process

- They address a question or problem.
- They think it through using the elements of reasoning.
- As they do this, they monitor their reasoning using the critical-thinking standards.

That's the core process of critical thinking, the heart of it. Critical thinkers who have never taken a course in critical thinking engage in this core process. They may not consciously name the elements as they think, they may not consider all the elements, they may not be explicitly aware that they are using the standards, but if you examine their reasoning, you will see that they are thinking about their purpose or their assumptions; they are considering alternatives; they are checking to be sure they are being accurate and that they have focused on the important parts of the problem.

Figure 5.1 offers a rough map of the core process, a blowup of the one introduced in Chapter 1. Now you should be in a better position to know what it's a map *of* and what the parts are. Figure 5.1 is just a rough map, of course. Thinking is not as linear as this implies: when you think through something critically, you don't necessarily start with the question (Q), *then* go to the elements, *then* go to the standards. You *can* think it out in that order if you wish, but the role of the standards is more of a persistent monitoring of your thinking. As you think through the question using the elements, you are striving to be clear, to stick to the important parts of the problem, to be accurate, to consider the problem sufficiently. Then, after you are done thinking through the problem, you use the standards again to check on your reasoning and sharpen it up. You ask yourself: "Okay, I tried to be accurate in what I was saying. Did I succeed? Do I need more evidence?" or: "I worked at being clear as I wrote my paper. But do I need to elaborate on what I said to make it clearer? Do I need another example, or maybe a contrasting example?"

The core process, then, involves questions, elements, and standards.

FIGURE 5.1 *The core process of critical thinking.*

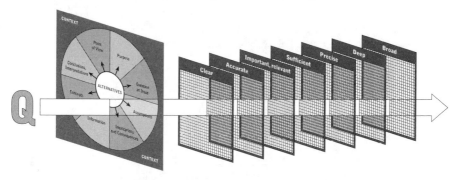

Doing More Than the Core Process

For some questions, however, you may have to do more than the core process.

The Core Process of Critical Thinking in a Discipline

If the question you are trying to address is one that's in the discipline, then you have to think it through using the *fundamental and powerful concepts* and relating it to the *central question* of that discipline. Ask yourself, "How do people in this discipline address such questions? How do they go about answering such questions?" If it's a question in anthropology, you need to engage in thinking anthropologically. If it's a question in engineering, you must think it through the way an engineer would. (See Chapter 2, pp. 50–51.)

Even if it's a question outside the discipline, about your personal life, or about some decision you have to make, it is reasonable to think it out from the point of view of disciplines that are relevant to that question. (See Chapter 2, pp. 77–78.) A fundamental thesis of this book is that thinking things through in terms of disciplines gives people *insight*. So, if you have a decision to make about diet, exercise, or smoking, it will help to ask, "How can I think this out biologically? nutritionally? medically?" You may also gain insight by asking, "How can I think it out psychologically? (How does my psychological way of thinking influence the decisions I make about dieting, exercise, smoking?) How can I think it out historically? (How does my society's history with regard to dieting, exercise, and smoking affect me and guide my choices?)" Marketing, math, sociology, literature: each of these, and many others, can not only help you understand the issues in a deep way, they can also help you make good decisions by showing possible courses of action and the influences that affect the success of those decisions.

We can envision the discipline as the lens of a telescope or microscope, as something we look through to focus our thinking in terms of the central concepts of that discipline (see Figure 5.2). We don't want to make the map more complicated, but we could easily add other lenses—other disciplines—as ways to gain further insight.

FIGURE 5.2 *The core process of critical thinking in a discipline.*

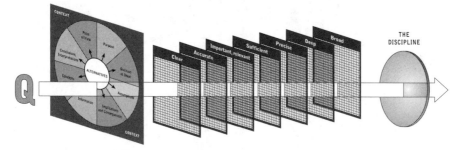

Thinking in Terms of Critical-Thinking Processes

There are other ways to do more than the core process. In the core process, you have already engaged in some specific critical-thinking processes. *Analysis* is a critical-thinking process of breaking something down into its component parts. You engaged in the process of analysis every time you broke something down into the elements of reasoning. At its root, analysis is going around the circle of elements. If you have gone around the circle with respect to a chapter in your text, you have analyzed it in terms of its purpose, its main question at issue, its main assumptions, and so on.

You haven't just broken the chapter down into its component parts, however. You have also gained an understanding of how those parts fit together into a coherent whole. In this book, we have been describing this whole as the logic of the question: after going around the circle, you have a good grasp of the logic of the chapter. This "bringing together into a whole" is often called the process of *synthesis*. So, in going around the circle, seeing each of the elements and grasping the logic of the question or topic, you have already been engaged in the critical thinking processes of *analyzing* and *synthesizing*. (See pp. 102–103.)

Depending on what is called for in the question, however, you still may have to do more than engage in the core process. You may have to engage in other processes besides analysis and synthesis. You may have to *compare and contrast* two different positions on euthanasia, for example. You may have to *evaluate* what a particular author says. You may need to *apply* a theory in the discipline to a new case. You may have to do some actual *decision making* about a course of action. You may have to engage in some *action*—writing a paper, performing the part of Mercutio, designing an experiment, even something as large-scale as starting a business. Notice that *action*—doing something—is classified here as a critical-thinking process. As with any of the other processes, you want your actions to be infused with your best thinking. All critical thinking involves doing something, but the other processes are things you do with your mind. The kind of action meant here is the kind that involves the whole person. That is, you may not just have to analyze how to diet, and make the decision to diet, you also actually have to *diet*—and you want that action, that doing, to be based on critical thinking.

Each of these critical-thinking processes is built from the elements and standards. We can add these critical thinking processes to the core process, as shown in Figure 5.3.

Doing Less than the Core Process

The core process is the centerpiece of critical thinking. Many times you have to do more than this core process just to address the various complexities of an issue. You may have to add the lenses of the disciplines themselves, and you may have to add other critical-thinking processes.

FIGURE 5.3 *Critical thinking processes.*

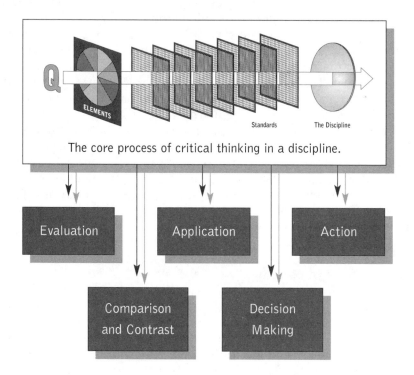

On the other hand, you often have to do *less* than the core process. You may take an author's position on animal rights and simply identify a crucial assumption behind it. Sometimes, that will be all that's necessary. The act of simply *identifying* a *single* element can be a deep insight in your critical thinking. Moreover, getting into the *habit* of identifying that single element can be a vital step in the development of your ability to think well. It can be valuable to you all by itself, without even considering the other elements.

Consider *purpose.* How many activities do you engage in where you lose sight of your purpose? Probably many of them. How many activities do you engage in where you dwell too heavily on *secondary* purposes—sometimes even letting them overwhelm the main purpose? For example, trying to earn grades, and forgetting the main reason you are in school; letting the guiding purpose in relationships become one of not getting into arguments; working to make a lot of money, but losing sight of what the money was ultimately for. Just getting into the habit of identifying your main purpose in activities that are important in your life can be a great benefit.

The same is true of each of the other elements. Simply focusing on anticipating the *consequences* of your decisions, for example, can make a crucial transformation in your life, especially if you can do it in a regular way. So can looking for *alternatives*. To a certain degree, this benefit can be independent of how you handle the other elements. Of course, your thinking may be deeper if you *also* pay attention to the other elements. Nevertheless, the act of focusing on consequences all by itself can change your thinking and actions in a dramatic way.

That is true for the standards as well. Consider accuracy. Here is a key sentence from a text on human population: "The linking of coal to iron has been second only to the development of agriculture in its impact upon the course of human history"[1] (by "the linking of coal to iron," the author means the mass production of steel). If you are asked: "What are the main developments that have influenced human history?" and you answer "the linking of coal to iron," you are accepting the claim as true. After a minute or two of reflecting about accuracy, however, you can probably think of many developments that were more influential than the mass production of steel on the course of human history (some possibilities: organized religion, language, the domestication of animals, the wheel, the development of democracy, road building). The claim seems clearly false, and just noticing its inaccuracy can open up a whole new avenue of thinking. It works in the other direction also: Antigone sees divine law and the ties of family as having more validity than the claims of human law; Creon sees human law as taking precedence over religious injunctions and family ties. Reflecting on the accuracy or inaccuracy of each of those principles can open up many profound truths.

For any given problem, the elements and standards are not all equally important. The decisions about which of them to focus on, whether to go all the way around the circle, or whether to engage in one or more of the other critical-thinking processes—all of these are themselves critical-thinking decisions.

Thinking Through Important Critical-Thinking Questions

Even with an overview and a series of maps, you may still be wondering *what to do* to think your way through a critical-thinking question in the discipline. How do you go about it? How do you start? How do you carry it through? How do you tell whether you have done it well? How do you improve? This chapter takes you through the basics of answering a critical-thinking question. It will also provide a more detailed exploration of putting it all together.

Below, in outline form, is the core process of critical thinking. It is an overview of putting it all together, thinking through an important critical-thinking question.

QEDS

Look at the <u>q</u>uestion.

Think it through using the <u>e</u>lements.

Think it through in terms of the <u>d</u>iscipline.

} Keep the <u>s</u>tandards in mind.

How to Start: Begin by Stepping Back

The most common ways to start thinking through a critical-thinking question are often not very effective. One standard way to start is just to start. I simply begin answering the question, relying on my mind to have sorted things out—or rather, *hoping* that my mind has sorted things out. Another common way to start is to look for information. I have to write a four-page paper about abortion. It has to have three references. So I scroll down the list of entries from my Internet search. I find three that look okay. I take a chunk of information from each and put it in my paper. I make sure it equals four pages.

A third standard way to begin is not to have the slightest idea how to begin. I wait until time pressure drives me to answer the question at the last minute. By that time the situation is desperate, so I'll be satisfied with just having something to turn in—anything. I can't afford the luxury of spending time trying to think things out.

There are more fruitful ways to think through a question and try to answer it. These ways begin with a central critical-thinking move: reflection. Take a metacognitive step, a step back. The question is in front of you. The natural impulse is to answer it, but don't do that yet. Instead, take a step back from the question, detach yourself from it. Don't ask yourself, "What is the answer?" Instead, ask yourself, "What is the question asking? What does it call for? What would I have to do in order to answer it?"

If you get the flavor of these stepping-back questions, you'll find that by thinking critically, you can construct a strategy for answering them.

Read the box on pp. 157–160. Then pick out some questions from your text. Choose some from later in the book, ones that come after chapters you have not read yet. Outline briefly what you need to do in order to answer those questions.

Try the same thing with two or three questions from other courses you are taking.

Later, at the end of this chapter, try the same activity again. Assess how much your abilities have improved.

Here are a few questions from textbooks in different fields, and how I might step back from them to see what I need to do to think through them critically. (These are not the only ways to approach these questions, of course, but they are good ways to start.) Notice that each of the responses focuses on *how* to answer the question critically, not on actually answering it.

1. Here is a question from a geography text. The text gives a half-page labeled "Critical Thinking: Tombouctoo." There are two paragraphs telling about the city of Tombouctoo (Timbuktoo), which was a fabulously rich, important urban market city on an ancient caravan route across the Sahara. Then the trade routes changed and Tombouctoo was bypassed; it's now a poor, mostly deserted city that plays no important role in today's world. The book then asks:

   > Compare Tombouctoo's location with that of Trabzon on the Black Sea in modern-day Turkey. Among which great empires was Trabzon once a major contact and trading point? How important is it today? Do you know of any other once-great cities that have declined as trade routes bypassed them?[2]

   What do I need to do to answer the question critically?

   a. Well, I know I'll need to read in the text about Trabzon. Even before reading, though, I can assume that Trabzon too was an urban trading center in a place where trade routes focused, and that it too was later bypassed. So, I will not simply be gathering information about Trabzon. I am thinking geographically: I am seeing that *place* (in this case, a city's position on a trade route) determines a great deal about that city—its prosperity, its origin, maybe its decline when bypassed. *Place* is a central concept in geography. So I am thinking in terms of a *system,* a *logic.* Figure 5.4 is a concept map of that system.

   b. As I step back from the question, I also start thinking about another one of the elements, *purpose:* Are most cities located in a certain place for the purpose of cornering trade on some trade route? Is that how cities are founded?

   (continued)

FIGURE 5.4 *A concept map of our critical thinking about Trabzon.*

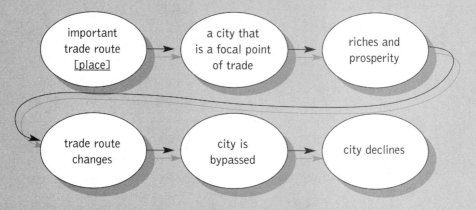

c. I further note that the question in the textbook asks me to engage in the critical-thinking process of *comparison*. So I will be looking for the important similarities between Trabzon and Tombouctoo. (I will also note relevant differences.)

d. The book then asks me to apply this geographical thinking to other once-great cities. For this, I can use my concept map. I begin at the beginning with once-important trade routes. Do I have any examples of that, either in my background knowledge or from other courses? (Some trade routes come to mind: there is the Oregon Trail; there is Route 66; there was the trade between Europe and America before the American Revolution.) I will then expect to find → cities that were a focal point of trade, that → achieved riches and prosperity, but → when trade routes changed, I should expect to find → cities that were bypassed and → then seriously declined. That is following the logic.

(There are implications of the critical thinking so far. I am surprised to find that a city's prosperity does not depend as heavily as I thought on the intelligence and individual business decisions of its inhabitants; those decisions, no matter how smart, may be overridden by the city's place on a bypassed trade route. It is even possible that

(continued)

I might later make a personal decision about where to live based partly on this geographical insight.)

2. Here is a question from a composition textbook. The question asks simply,

What is your definition of obscenity?[3]

Then you are directed to read a paragraph that quotes various Supreme Court justices saying that they can recognize obscenity even without an adequate definition. The paragraph also contains the current Supreme Court criteria for obscenity: "a work must be 'patently offensive' and lack artistic, literary, political, or scientific value to be declared legally obscene" (p. 128).

As I step back from the question, I notice that it does not mention any standards. It's not reasonable, however, to conclude that no standards are intended. Any definition I end up giving should be *accurate* and as *clear* as possible.

I step back and ask: What makes for a good *definition?* What is the logic of definitions? It won't be enough just to give my off-hand opinion of obscenity, or just give an example. It has to be a *definition.*

I know there are two major sides to this issue of obscenity. To address the question, I need to feel the pull of free speech and the need for free expression. There is a logic, a system, to that way of thinking. But I also feel the pull of those who are offended by obscenity, those who feel children and others can be harmed by it. There is a logic to that way of thinking also. Regardless of which side I am on, I need to write out the logic of both points of view.

3. Here are two history questions. In the text they are called Review Questions:

How did some Americans resist the rapid changes taking place in the post-World War I world? What cultural and political strategies did they use?[4]

(continued)

This looks like a question requiring only recall on my part. If I happen to know some details from lectures or on my own, fine, but that's not expected. I will just find the place in the book where this topic is talked about, so that I can "review" it. I still have to make a judgment about which cultural and political strategies were most important, but critical-thinking skills are not needed to answer the question.

There is not much opportunity here to think the way a historian does. Historians seldom simply repeat an account given by others. Instead, they rethink that account—they look for implications; they give interpretations; they try to make their understanding deeper, more comprehensive. The field of history is a lot more exciting and creative than simply regurgitating information.

I could do some historical critical thinking about the question. I could ask:

- What in the American experience does this illuminate?
- What are some other examples of resistance to rapid change in earlier chapters?
- What are some examples from my own time? How are they similar?
- What are some reasonable ways to adapt to a rapidly changing society? Can I find historical examples of those ways? What criteria have people used in the past?

4. The next question in the same history text is:

Discuss the 1928 election as a mirror of the divisions in American society.

Since it asks me to "discuss," it looks like it might call for critical thinking. Really, though, it's merely asking me to repeat a "discussion" already given in the book. It is just a pseudo–critical-thinking question. If I'm going to think critically about the divisions in American society, I'll have to do it on my own.

Q. Looking at the Question

Three Categories of Questions

A major help in seeing how to answer a critical-thinking question comes when you think in terms of how many "systems" you need to use in order to answer it. First, though, a little background.

Traditionally, questions can be classified into three categories: those that call for *facts* as answers; those that call for *mere opinions, reactions,* or *mere preferences* as answers; and those that call for *reasoned judgments* as answers. Here are a few examples of each.

- Questions that call for statements of fact:

  What is the atomic mass of hydrogen?

  What are the five most populous countries in the world today?

  Find the slope of the line by solving for y: $2x + 6y = 5$.

- Questions that call for statements of mere opinion or subjective preferences:

  Who is your favorite character in *To Kill a Mockingbird?*

  What was your reaction to *Shakespeare in Love?*

- Questions that call for reasoned judgment:

  In what major ways did Leonardo embody the spirit of the Renaissance?

  How can I improve my test scores in my political science class?

  Which air-conditioning system should I use in my house?

As far as critical thinking is concerned, the most important of these categories is the one calling for reasoned judgment. Facts are part of answering most critical-thinking questions, but they will usually not be the answer all by themselves. Personal preferences can also be important for answering a critical-thinking question. If you are trying to decide which area of the country to live in, clearly you need to consult your personal preferences about the kind of environment you like. You also need facts: data from a reputable source about the areas of the country you are considering. But the question itself will call for *reasoned judgment:* how to interpret the factual data, how to apply it to your personal preferences, what other likely consequences there will be of living in that locale, what alternatives there are.

This way of classifying questions is only a rough one, not entirely satisfactory.[5] Richard Paul has refined it by changing the focus. His focus is not on the kind of *answer* a question requires (e.g., fact, preference, reasoned judgment). Instead, he focuses on the *procedure* you would use to answer that question. Specifically, he talks about the number of *systems* you would use to think through the question reasonably.

A good way to begin reasoning through a question, then, is to classify it as falling into one of these categories:

Category 1 questions require you to think out an answer by using *only one system*. (This category will include many factual-type questions.)

Category 2 questions require *no system* to reason them out. (This category will include most personal-preference and subjective-reaction questions.)

Category 3 questions require you to think them out using *more than one system*. (This category will include most questions that call for reasoned judgment.)[6]

CATEGORY 1. Here are some examples:

Question: What are the five most populous countries in the world today?
What **system** is it reasonable to use to answer it? → You look it up in a reliable source.

Question: Find the slope of the line by solving for y: $2x + 6y = 5$.
What **system** is it reasonable to use to answer it? → You follow the mathematical system for solving for y.

Question: How do you conjugate a *regular* verb in French?
System to use? → You use the rule or pattern for that type of regular verb.

Question: How do you conjugate an *irregular* verb in French?
System to use? → There may be no rule that lets you figure it out. So, the system is initially to look it up in your French book. Afterward, if possible, you will internalize the conjugation of that verb through a combination of memorizing and repeated practice. After you internalize it, the system you'll use to conjugate the verb will become whether it sounds right to your ear or looks right on the page.

Question: An exercise from a composition text: "Identify and correct any comma splices in the following paragraph."
System to use? → You look up "comma splice" in the index and apply the rule to the paragraph. Or, you have already internalized the rule: you check the system "in your head."

Question: What is the atomic mass of hydrogen?
System to use? → You calculate it, using the formula.
Alternative system to use → You look it up on the periodic table.

Notice some features of Category 1 questions:

a. Though many of the answers are facts, not all are.

b. They can require different degrees of thinking. If you haven't internalized the concept of comma splice, you'll have to go through the laborious process of finding the rule in the book, identifying the relevant part of the rule, and applying it to the paragraph or to your writing. That can be time consuming. If you have internalized comma splice, on the other hand, it's as if you don't have to think about it at all: you just "see" that the comma is wrong there. In time you may forget about the rule entirely, and "automatically" write complete sentences.

c. Category 1 questions are not always easy, but—once you realize that they are single-system questions—they are often easier than they look. You may not like problem solving in math, but for people who do, a truly satisfying feeling comes from knowing that following the rules makes even difficult problems solvable. You may remember the teacher in the movie *Stand and Deliver* who taught his high school students to do calculus as Category 1 questions. No matter how difficult the problem looked, all they had to do was apply the rules.

An effective system for answering Category 1 questions is to look them up in a reliable source. What source would you consult to find out facts about evolution, a creationist, an evolutionary biologist, someone midway between the two?

Thus, once you classify a question as falling into Category 1, it gives you something useful: a way to go about answering the question. In each case, you answer the question by first *identifying* the single system you should use, and, second, by *applying* that system to the problem at hand.

CATEGORY 2. A no-system question is one that calls for mere preferences, mere personal opinions, or mere reactions. The word "mere" is important for getting the feel of this category. An example is: "Who is your favorite character in *To Kill a Mockingbird?*" Notice that, taking the question literally, your answer does not even need to be defended, and your favorite character might change from moment to moment. You *merely* have to report who your favorite character is. Moreover, since critical-thinking questions are always ones that can be reasoned out well or poorly, Category 2 questions are not really critical-thinking questions at all. You can't really get your favorite character "wrong," or even reason it out better or worse: it's simply a preference, a reaction.

Here is a question from a literature text.[8] It follows a short essay by Bill Cosby:

> "How does Cosby use specific examples to create humor? Is his humor effective? Explain your answer."

Focus on the second question in particular: How could you read that as a Category 2 question? Is it, in your best judgment, a Category 2 question? Why or why not?

In practice, though, teachers and texts sometimes ask questions that *look* as though they are in Category 2, but they should be interpreted as Category 3. A questioner's purpose can often be as important for interpreting a question as the words used, and sometimes this means not taking the question too literally. Here is a question from a text in education:

> Bill [in a case study of how he taught his junior high school social studies class] wanted his students to learn about the Battle of the Little Bighorn from various cultural viewpoints. Do you think he was correct in doing this?[7]

Taken literally, you could answer this in a single word: Yes, No, Maybe. But it wouldn't be a reasonable interpretation. The questioner clearly wants you to discuss reasons for or against, and then to evaluate those reasons. The question may also be a loaded one: the text is strongly *in favor of* what Bill did, in favor of teaching about controversial events from various cultural viewpoints. That does not necessarily make it biased: valuing culturally diverse points of view seems a reasonable approach to teaching, and the text supports this approach with reasons. However, you do need to take this context into account when you interpret the question. If you conclude that Bill's decision was *incorrect*, you will need to give considerably more support than if you agree with Bill.

Some things to notice about Category 2 questions:

a. Mere preferences and reactions are never the only factor in a critical-thinking decision, but they are often important. If you love raw oysters, a mere preference, then other things being equal, that is a good reason for eating raw oysters. But other things have to be equal. That's where critical thinking comes in. Before you make the decision, you need the reasonable conviction that other factors, like health hazards, do not outweigh the preference.

b. Though there is no system for answering Category 2 questions—you merely state preferences or reactions—there may well be a system to explaining the *causes* of those preferences and reactions. That is a question often explored in the social and natural sciences, business, and the arts. People in these fields search, for example, for psychological, economic, and biological explanations for why people have the reactions they do: why we like or dislike oysters, why we love the people we love, why we prefer movies with sex and violence. But unlike the reactions themselves, these are deep questions in the disciplines, and they are definitely not Category 2 questions.

c. Here is a complication to the story. There is evidence that for some mere reactions, it can take considerable skill just to identify them. Thus, people sometimes feel emotions that they don't know they are feeling. Some children are taught that it is bad to feel anger, for example; other children are taught that they shouldn't be afraid. They learn these lessons so well that even as adults they are not able to tell that they are angry or afraid—or they can tell only when the emotions become extreme, or in socially acceptable situations. The same is true of mere preferences. Sometimes we can be so brainwashed by hearing about what we are *supposed to* prefer, that it can blind us to what we *in fact* prefer. So at some level there may be critical-thinking skills involved even in identifying our mere preferences and reactions, especially if they are subtle or less than fully conscious.

Hasn't it happened to you that other people could tell you were angry when you yourself didn't know it? Maybe you even felt sure you were not angry. (You said, stonily, "I am *not* angry!") Only later did you realize that in fact you were.

Do you always automatically know what your reactions and preferences are?

CATEGORY 3. To answer Category 3 questions, you have to think in terms of *more than one system.*

Take a simple ethical dilemma as an example. You are a parent, and you wonder whether to tell your young child that there is no Santa Claus. You feel the pull of two systems. One system centers around the importance of honesty; the other centers around the importance of preserving the magic of childhood. This is not a battle simply between one *principle* and another. Rather, each principle is a *system*; each has a logic you can think in terms of. What is your concept of honesty? Why is it important? What are its limits? The same questions apply to the importance of preserving the magic of childhood.

To answer this Category 3 question critically, then, you have to think it through using *both* systems.

This is a very simple issue, but the same idea runs through all Category 3 questions. Thinking through an issue critically requires that you feel the pull of the different systems involved in the question. Then, it requires you to weigh the importance of each, and give each system an adequate voice. Maybe you can come to a definite conclusion about the issue, maybe not. But the heart of addressing a Category 3 question is thinking it through in terms of different systems.

Think of the question on p. 159 about defining obscenity. To think through this issue critically, you must think in terms of at least two different systems, one centering around free speech and the other centering around people's desire to be protected from what is offensive to them. If you write an essay on obscenity and think it through using *only one* of these systems, it will be seriously flawed as a piece of critical thinking. You treated a Category 3 question as if it were a Category 1 question. That would automatically diminish the quality of your response.

The word "system" is a good one because it is so flexible. Consider how it applies to a range of examples.

Question: How can I improve my test scores in my political science class?

Systems to think in terms of: You need to think this out in terms of the type of test the teacher gives in this course and the study strategy that fits that type of test. The way tests and strategies fit together is system #1. Thus, if the test is one that emphasizes sheer recall of individual facts, a good strategy might be to SEIE important terms (see pp. 170–171), to memorize them using flash cards, or (most effectively) to understand them in terms of the f&p concepts of the discipline and the central question of the course. On the other hand, if the test requires overall understanding and reasoning in the discipline, memorizing won't work at all. A good strategy would be to engage in critical reading of the text and critical listening during class discussion, and to spend study time outlining in terms of f&p concepts and the central question.

System #2 centers around *you,* what your study strengths and weaknesses are, the amount of time you're willing to invest in improving your test scores in this class, what is feasible to do in the amount of time you have.

Question: In what major ways did Leonardo embody the spirit of the Renaissance?

Systems to think in terms of: System #1: how Leonardo thought, wrote, lived, and painted—the system that unifies these. I need to grasp the logic of this. I can't just begin writing or just collect information. Next I have to think of system #2, the Renaissance: its values, its tendencies, how it differed from other periods. It is clear that this is a *system* because I could use this Renaissance way of thinking to address topics we have never considered in class. With a solid grasp of that system, I could try to describe how a Renaissance person would think about almost anything—clothes, money, business, travel. Specifically, I could see how much of this system, the spirit of the Renaissance, fits in with the system I saw in Leonardo.

If this is a piece of writing I have to do about Leonardo and the Renaissance, or a presentation in class, thinking it out as a Category 3 question, in terms of *systems*, provides a logical outline of how to go about it effectively and practically. I'll have to do *research*—but I realize by now that research is not just information-gathering. It is gathering information as it is linked together by a *system* or *logic*. In this case, it's both those systems described previously, plus a third—the way they fit together.

Question: Decide on an air-conditioning system for your house.

Systems to think in terms of: square footage (calculate this); cooling capacity of various units (research this); performance information (*Consumer Reports?*); your finances.

Thinking in terms of systems, using reasoned judgment to weigh the pull of one system against another, is the heart of answering Category 3 questions in disciplines. In each family of disciplines we are required to do something similar: to think in terms of the various systems that are central to that discipline, how those systems interact, modify one another, sometimes conflict. We also must think in terms of the systems in the world that the discipline investigates.

Learning to classify questions into these categories, right at the start, is an extremely useful skill to develop. It cuts away extraneous factors and focuses us on exactly those systems that will be most useful in answering the question.

Q: Looking at the Question: A Flow Chart

Classify the question as Category 1, Category 2, or Category 3.

CATEGORY 1: It can be answered using a single system.

→ Identify the system you need to use.

→ Apply the system to the question at issue.

→ Infuse it with more critical thinking by asking questions in terms of the elements and standards.

CATEGORY 2: No system is needed.

- It is not a critical-thinking question → state (and explain) your preference or your reaction.
- Interpret it as a critical-thinking question → classify it as Category 1 or Category 3.

CATEGORY 3: It requires thinking in more than one system.

→ First, identify the most important systems you need to use to answer the question. (Actively look for the different systems within the question.)

→ Second, think the question out using each important system. (Follow out implications, explore purposes, note other key questions that arise, identify underlying assumptions, set the thinking in context: work through elements and standards as needed.)

→ Finally, come to the most reasonable overall conclusion you can, bringing the systems together in the most appropriate way.

E. Thinking It Through Using the Elements

So, you start off with a question to answer. You interpret it. You identify the system or systems you need to use to answer it. You apply these to the question.

Maybe you're done.

If it's a Category 1 or Category 2 question, you may indeed be done, especially if it's an unimportant one. If it is a Category 3 question, probably you're not done.

What do you do now?

You have to use the elements of reasoning. As Chapter 3 emphasized, the elements are the nuts and bolts of critical thinking. (In fact, you used them when you thought things out in terms of systems.) You have to think out the question or problem in terms of the elements: go around the circle. (See pp. 102–103.)

Some Questions Need to Be Thought Through Fully

Depending on the importance of the question, you may spend considerable time on each of the elements. In any event, spend the time you need on each of them. If some elements are problematic, you can put them aside until later. Apply the elements flexibly; maybe to one system, maybe to both, maybe to the way they come together in the question. Your flexibility is guided by your judgment of what is relevant to the specific question at issue.

Suppose the question you are considering is important to you. Maybe it's a paper, a major assignment, a presentation in class, your preparation for an essay exam. Maybe it's something that's important to you personally or professionally—a decision about how to budget your time between work, school, family, and recreation; or a business decision; or a client, patient, or student who does not fit the usual profile and requires special help.

You need go around the whole circle.

Why? For two reasons. Though the elements are not all equally important in any given problem, any one of them could turn out to be crucial for this problem. Going around the circle can give you the insight you need into the question and how to answer it. The second reason is that this is an *important question* to you. You need to give it the time and attention it deserves in your thinking. By devoting the concentrated thought process of going around the circle to the best of your ability, you are showing respect for the importance of this question in your life. Major decisions *merit* major thought processes.

There is a third reason as well, one that just has to do with developing your critical-thinking skills. The more the elements become ingrained in your thinking, the better you'll become as a critical thinker. That requires practice. It would be beneficial if they could become as natural as looking where you're going when you drive. If you're practicing the elements, you may spend only a minute or so on each, but try to make that minute a *focused* minute with your attention riveted on that element as it applies to the question.

After going around the circle, take the time to do some *synthesis.* The question, what is involved in it, and the answer as you see it are all there in your analysis. Reassemble the pieces—the elements as applied to the question—into a coherent whole. Step back once again to gain a perspective on the logic of the question and your answer to it.

Some Questions Do Not Need to Be Thought Through Fully

Maybe the question you're addressing is not such an important one; maybe it doesn't need to be treated as fully. Maybe, as you read it, one, two, or three of the elements jump out as the ones you should focus on. You don't *always* have to go around the full circle.

Here is an example (several others are given in the exercises). A sociology text contains a short essay on how the process of being socialized limits our freedom. It then asks:

Do you think our society affords more freedom to males than to females? Why or why not?[9]

A critical-thinking response: In terms of the elements, *concept* stands out from the question: What is the concept of freedom that is being asked about? What kind of freedom? You may get different answers depending on the kind of freedom you focus on. You'll want to be as clear and precise about that as possible, and discuss two or three different kinds of freedom.

Another element stands out: *point of view*. Be sure to give full weight to both male and female points of view. You especially need to be acutely aware of your own gender biases (maybe unconscious ones) that may creep in.

A third element stands out: *information*. You can give a thoughtful, balanced answer to this question or just shoot from the hip. Everyone has an impression about this gender question, but this is a *sociology course*, not a place to trade unsupported opinions. You need to find information that is as accurate and up-to-date as possible.

S: Using the Standards

The standards are the subject of Chapter 4, and are addressed briefly here. A standards check appears on pp. 144–145, and on pp. 140–141 there is a series of questions on evaluating around the circle. Both are ways to evaluate and improve your thinking.

You use the standards essentially in two ways:

- *while* you are answering a question, and
- *afterward*, when you are checking your work, or revising it to make it better.

Like the elements, the standards are something you need to internalize. That comes as you practice using them, especially as you consciously and explicitly practice using them. You will be better at some standards than others, and that can change from one topic to another.

Internalizing and incorporating *even one* standard into your way of thinking can substantially improve your thinking everywhere. Take clearness. There are two aspects to clearness: getting clear in your own thinking and presenting your thinking clearly to others (see pp. 118–120). Anne Buchanan teaches high school biology. Teachers in her state (Kentucky) must give proof that they have covered the National and State Requirements of Core Content. This core content consists of 80 core statements (for example, "DNA is used to direct the synthesis of proteins"). She has students take each of the 80 and "SEIE them."[10] SEIE is a technique for making something clearer:

S: State it.

E: Elaborate [explain it more fully, and in other words].

I: Illustrate [give an illustration].

E: Exemplify [give an example].

When the students SEIE the 80 statements, the teacher has proof that she has covered those statements. But, more than that, she can also prove unequivocally that her students *understand* them. For any subject matter you study, if you can get yourself in the habit of making it clearer using SEIE, you will dramatically improve your thinking. Similarly, in your presentations (papers, exams, reports, oral presentations), if you clarify what you say by elaborating on it, giving illus- trations and examples, your presentations will improve dramatically.

D: Thinking It Through in Terms of the Discipline

Addressing the question using the lens of the discipline is the fourth part of the core process of critical thinking:

Q

E

D
} S

It is important to remember, though, that these are not steps you do in *sequence*. You may do them sequentially for a course, by taking a process you already engage in and breaking it down into the parts **Q-E-D-S**. But when you think critically, you use them all, and you use them in an interwoven way. So, knowing that this step is not fully distinct from elements and standards, how do you answer a question by thinking it through in terms of the discipline?

As we are putting it all together, we can focus on three key ways to think questions through in terms of the discipline. Each of them involves a different approach, but all of them overlap to a consider- able degree:

- systems
- fundamental and powerful concepts in the discipline
- the central question of the discipline.

Systems

When you classify a question as Category 1, 2, or 3, you gain an impor- tant insight into how to approach it: it leads you to identify the *system* (or systems) implicit in the question. In a straightforward way, thinking a question through in terms of the discipline means learning to think in terms of the main systems that are used in that discipline. If it's called for in the question, you need to know how to solve for x, iden- tify the most populous countries, find the atomic mass of hydrogen, or conjugate a French verb. You need to be able to think in terms of the

Renaissance in history, in terms of business systems, health-related systems, any of the systems that are called for in the question.

Part of thinking in systems is knowing the standard way that type of question is addressed in that discipline. There is a variety of systems, but here are some examples, together with some of the disciplines they might apply to. (Of course, in all disciplines, in all systems, you have to *reason* your way to an answer.) You might

- use well-established theories and laws (sciences)
- use highly respected points of view within the discipline (literary criticism, art theories)
- use case studies and expert practice (business, health sciences)
- use experiments and their findings (social sciences)
- use opposing points of view (philosophy, political science)

All of these clearly involve thinking things through in terms of systems in the discipline.

F&P Concepts, Central Question

Recall that f&p concepts are those basic concepts that lie at the heart of a discipline or course (see pp. 59–62). (As a reminder, examples might be: homeostasis in biology, Romanticism in literature, supply and demand in economics.) The *central question* of the course is usually closely related: it is *the* most central question that the course is addressing (see pp. 65–68). This book speaks of *the* central question as if there were only one, and that is the ideal case. There may in fact be several closely related central questions, but there cannot be many. (A biology example might be, "How do living things work?" Or, breaking that down only a little further, "How does the body work?" "How did organisms come to be the way they are [the origin of species]?" "How are life-forms in a community interdependent?") It is a major goal of the course that you incorporate those f&p concepts and central questions into your thinking patterns.

In an earlier example we worked through a geography question about Tombouctoo, about cities on trade routes. We worked it through using the system that was shown in Figure 5.4:

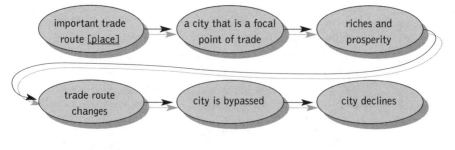

F&p concepts sometimes sound particularly lame or trivial when you write them down. "Place" may seem that way. Part of what makes concepts fundamental and powerful is that they are deep. So you have to make a conscious effort to see them as deep. "Place" can seem trivial, but it can be incredibly deep: Without being a geographer, it's hard to comprehend just how fundamental and powerful it is, how much of people's lives—how they live, what they do for a living, whom they marry, when they die—is determined by *place.*

Probably the most fundamental and powerful concept in geography is *place* or *the influence of place.* So, as you think the answer out in terms of this specific system, you are asking yourself:

How does the influence of place determine the fate of cities?

You have already been addressing this question, but in a much more specific way, when you reasoned out how changing trade routes affect the prosperity of cities. But thinking it out explicitly in terms of place is much more conscious—and much more fundamental and powerful. Now, your answer to this question will relate to all the other topics you have learned to think out in terms of *place.* Instead of this being merely one specific system (amid hundreds of other specific systems), all the geographical systems you use are unified by the f&p concept of *place.* Not only are cities' fates influenced by their *place* on a trade route, but our lives in countless dimensions are also heavily influenced by *where* we live them.

This is thinking geographically. It is thinking the way a geographer thinks. Geographers interpret the world around them in terms of *place:* you can ask them a question, not just about Tombouctoo, but about Washington, D. C. or Los Angeles or the city you live in, and they will see what happens there as a function of that city's place: weather, ecosystem, topography, cultural diffusion, and population patterns.

The same is true for the central question. As you think through specific systems, or research some specific information, you relate it to the central question in the course. The central question and the f&p concepts are usually closely linked. The central question in a geography course might be:

How does the geography of where something happens influence *what* happens?

As you use the core process of critical thinking in the discipline, you think the question out in terms of

- systems (these may be very specific)
- f&p concepts ⎫ through these I see the question
- central questions ⎭ in the context of the whole

Why Use F&P Concepts and Central Questions?

So why do this? You've used a system to answer the question, maybe more than one system. You've *been* thinking in terms of the discipline. Why would you add to your work by thinking it through using f&p concepts?

First, though it is more work in the short run, it's not *much* more work. It just looks like more on paper, and because you're not used to it. It is really a shift in emphasis. Sometimes answering the question in terms of f&p concepts comes in just a flash of realization, an Aha! After you get used to this way of thinking, it will make *all* the questions in the discipline much more answerable. In fact, it will *cut down* on the work you have to do. What *is* work is memorizing and retaining a hundred different pieces of information or thinking through a hundred unrelated specific systems. Many of those—maybe all of them—can be thought through far more efficiently using f&p concepts and central questions.

But the main reason to use f&p concepts is that this *is* the work of thinking in terms of the discipline. The specific system you think through—explaining the decline of Tombouctoo, for example, or calculating the atomic mass of hydrogen—isn't the discipline. Each specific system is only a small fragment of the discipline. To think geographically or chemically, however, is to give yourself an insight into a whole range of questions and answers.

It is like all of critical thinking in that respect. It *is* an effort, especially before you get used to it. But, it has clear practical benefits that far exceed the effort. It will produce better answers, better grades, in more courses, in more professions, with ultimately less work, than any alternative. More than that, it gives insight that can make your life richer, by bringing the elements, the standards, and the disciplines into how you think things through.

The exercises to Chapter 5 are geared to addressing questions in your specific discipline or disciplines. Those questions will be everywhere: asked in the text, asked by your instructor, by fellow students, by you. Some will be unasked but implicit in the readings and the class experience. You need to practice analyzing and answering these using **QEDS** within the discipline, and you need to receive feedback from classmates and from instructors.

5.1 Go around the circle in the discipline; do a standards check.

   a. Go around the circle with respect to the discipline as a whole. Make this a pre-test: keep your answer, but don't look at it during the semester. Repeat this analysis near the end of the course as a post-test; do a standards check; compare the two; assess how your understanding of the discipline has changed and deepened.

   b. Go around the circle with respect to an important subdiscipline in your field (e.g., if your discipline is *psychology*, → analyze *experimental psych*, or *social psych*, etc; *business* → *marketing, accounting*, etc.). Do a standards check.

   c. Go around the circle with respect to the family of disciplines yours belongs to (e.g., social sciences, natural sciences, arts, humanities, business.). Do a standards check.

   d. Go around the circle with respect to this book on thinking critically. Do a standards check.

Instructions for Exercises 5.2 through 5.6: Classify the question as Category 1, 2, or 3. Briefly describe the system or systems you would use to think it through to a reasonable answer. If it is Category 1 or 2, identify some questions you could ask to infuse it with more critical thinking.

5.2 A question from a biology text:

   If all organisms had not descended from a common ancestor, and did not possess many common genes and mechanisms of development, would we be able to perform valid medical research [for humans] using mice and in some case, *Drosophila*? Why or why not?[11]

   [*Drosophila*, I find out from the text, are fruit flies.]

5.3 A book on the history of the arts:

SUMMARY. After reading this chapter you should be able to:

- Identify and explain the political and religious conditions that led to the Reformation, including the theological and dogmatic contentions of Erasmus, Luther, Zwingli, Calvin, and Montaigne.[12]

5.4 A question on a legal case from a business law text:

Intoxication. Betty Galloway, an alcoholic, signed a settlement agreement upon her divorce from her husband, Henry Galloway. Henry, in Betty's absence in court, stated that she had lucid intervals from her alcoholism, had been sober for two months, and was lucid when she signed the settlement agreement on September 22, 1978. Betty moved only to vacate the settlement agreement on September 27, 1978, after she had retained present legal counsel. On January 23, 1979, Betty was declared incompetent to handle her person and affairs, and a guardian and conservator was appointed. Betty, through her guardian, sued to have the settlement agreement voided. Who wins? [*Galloway v. Galloway*, 281 N.W.2d 804 (N.D. 1979)][13]

5.5 One of 15 fill-in-the-blank questions in a chapter in an astronomy book:

Ishtar Terra and Aphrodite Terra are two _____ on the surface of Venus.[14]

5.6 Someone asks you to give your reaction to the question of abortion.

5.7 Analyze the following passage in terms of the elements and standards. It is a paragraph from the constitution of the Islamic Republic of Iran:

The family unit is the foundation of society and the main institution for the growth and advancement of mankind. . . . It is the principal duty of the Islamic government to regard women as the unifying factor of the family unit and its position. They are a factor in bringing the family out of the service of propagating consumerism and exploitation and renewing the vital and valuable duty of motherhood in raising educated human beings. . . . As a result motherhood is accepted as a most profound responsibility in the Muslim viewpoint and will, therefore, be accorded the highest value and generosity.[15]

5.8 My geology text lists 28 "important terms" and 14 main points of "summary" for Chapter 2 alone. Chapter 2 is on minerals. Chapter 3 (on igneous rocks) lists 35 additional "important terms" and 15 main points of "summary." That's in 46 pages of the book, and there are over 600 pages all together. At this rate, by the end of the book I'll have to know almost 800 important terms and around 400 main points of summary. What can I do?

5.9 What elements would you focus on to answer the following question from a literature text? It follows a story by Ernest Hemingway, "The Short Happy Life of Francis Macomber," and it asks a question about the three main characters.

> What do Wilson, Francis, and Margot each think it means to be a real man? What would you guess Hemingway thinks?[16]

5.10 Take some important paragraphs from readings in your course. Analyze them in terms of the elements and standards (as in Exercise 5.7).

5.11 Look at the questions that arise in your course. Classify them as Category 1, 2, or 3. If they are Category 1 or 2, ask questions about elements or standards to infuse them with critical thinking. If they are Category 3 questions, identify the systems you need to think in terms of to answer them.

5.12 Using the information from Exercise 5.11, feel the pull of each system. Adequately describe each. Finally, answer the questions.

5.13 In your text or the course as a whole, find an issue, problem, or critical-thinking question important enough to merit going around the full circle. Then, do the analysis and synthesis by going around the circle. Do a standards check.

5.14 Look carefully at some critical-thinking questions in your subject textbook. Identify the elements of reasoning that stand out and must be addressed in answering the question.

5.15 Group work.   Answer with critical thinking.

Sit in groups of four:

A asks a question in the discipline or related to it.

The group gets two minutes for thinking.

B classifies the question as Category 1, 2, or 3.

C describes the systems that need to be thought through to answer the question.

D explains which elements need to be addressed to answer it.

A (having taken some notes) does a standards check on B's, C's, and D's responses.

Switch roles.

5.16 **Group work.**   Discuss critically:

- How does Figure 5.2 work? How does it describe critical thinking?
- How much work will it take to engage in critical thinking in this course?
- To what extent will it save work?
- Will it transfer to other courses? to day-to-day life?

Responses to Starred (*) Exercises

Chapter 1

1.3 In almost any large group, the same answers occur: most people think that *others* are heavily influenced by advertising and conform a great deal, but that they themselves are influenced and conform only a little, maybe not at all. Almost all people think that they are better than average drivers.

There is clearly something off-kilter about this. People in general cannot be right about themselves. *Are* people heavily influenced even though they believe they are not? Are *you* heavily influenced even though you believe you are not?

1.4a From a critical-thinking point of view, essential questions to raise are ones (i) about *clearness:* "What does this mean? What are the implications of saying the U.S. is #1?" (ii) about *precision:* "Number one in what respect?" and (iii) about *importance:* "Why does it matter if the U.S. is number one in some respects?"

1.6 Here are three of my questions:

- Will the same film be there with all shampoos, even the store's?
- Is the film the result of the shampoo or of something else entirely?
- Is there anything negative about having that film on my hair that can only be seen with a microscope?

Note: You probably came up with these questions or with others just as good. That is a good critical-thinking response. But you were prompted by this book, and so it isn't an "authentic" problem—either for you or for me. The real issue is: Would you—or I—have actually asked questions like that if we were the ones getting the haircut? Would it have occurred to us to ask questions like these?

1.9 Here are some possible criteria you could have used:

I thought it through critically because I

- realistically assessed my need for something
- gathered sufficient information to make the best decision

- asked the important questions beforehand.

I did not think it through critically because I

- engaged in wishful thinking
- went along without asking the questions I needed to ask
- put what I wanted at the moment over what was really important to me.

Actually, the most common criterion people give is not a reasonable one at all. People often judge whether they reasoned something out *well* by whether it *turned out well*, and they conclude that they failed to reason something out well because it *turned out badly*.

But those are not reasonable criteria. A decision can turn out well or badly because of circumstances we have no way of knowing about. I may make a bad decision and have it happen to turn out well. If I make the most reasonable decision available under the circumstances, it is still the most reasonable decision even if it turns out badly.

Check your answers to see if you used this unreasonable criterion.

1.12 There could be many good hypotheses, and they can be different depending on where you live. (In New Orleans, one hypothesis would be that a festival is taking place in the French Quarter.) But this is intended as a question about egocentricity. Your list should contain the following hypothesis as a prominent possibility: *You* are the one who is driving erratically (and that makes it look as though everyone else is).

1.15 Here's an example.

Situation: I'm considering dropping this course because it looks too hard.

Question: What *assumptions* am I making about this situation?
Answer: I am assuming it will be too hard → I wonder if that's accurate?

Question: What *conclusion* should I draw about this situation?
Answer: My conclusion is to wait and see. I need more information.

Question: What are some other *points of view* that might help?
Answer: I could discuss it with the teacher. Maybe she can't help, but maybe she can. It won't hurt to try.

1.16 Maybe the person wrote down only vague, easy-going comments. This is a very common response. Some possible conclusions you might draw are that the person values being nice, that the person wants to avoid hurting your feelings (whether your feelings would in fact be hurt or not), that the person wants to avoid any possibility of conflict, and that the person has not thought of any more focused comments to make.

Chapter 2

2.2a Here is the way the authors reason: They start with a general point (a piece of information) about communicating effectively. Then they make their point clearer by defining a key term: audience. Next, they become more precise, by specifying types of audiences. In paragraph 2 they focus on important questions at issue you need to raise. Finally, in the last sentence, they draw out an implication for how you can make better decisions about writing for an audience. (*Information, question at issue,* and *implication* are all elements of reasoning; *clear, precise,* and *important* are all standards of critical thinking.)

2.4 It seems to make good sense: the argument is saying that 10,000 miles is too far for hunter-gatherers to have traveled in a mere 2,000 years.

It makes sense until you think mathematically. That's only 5 miles per year. That's not far at all.

2.6 This is a response only to the example part of the question. There are examples of actions that are legal but unethical: adultery is legal; lying is legal (except on contracts); breaking your promises is legal. There are also actions that are ethical but illegal (Rosa Parks's refusal to give up her seat on the bus).

So your explanation of the difference between ethical and legal thinking should fit examples like these.

2.8 Here's my concept map:

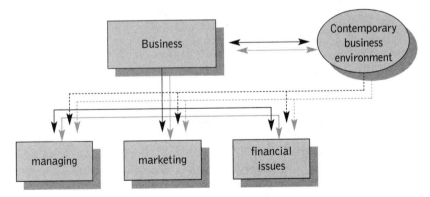

The f&p concepts of the book as a whole are the three rectangles directly under "Business," plus the oval off to the side. To call them f&p concepts is to say this: take any problem in business, and try to think it out in terms of managing, marketing, and financial issues, and apply those in the context of the contemporary business environment. I put this last concept in an oval to signify to myself that it operates in a different way from the other three.

2.13 One such map is the one in Figure 1.3, at the end of Chapter 1.

2.14 The new paradigm highlights *plan, organize,* and *lead*—but to achieve *what*? That "what" is an f&p concept that's missing. If I am going to think managerially, I have to think not just in terms of planning, organizing, and leading, but in terms of the *goals* these are intended to achieve. (Notice how actual managers can lose sight of this *goal* concept.)

2.16 The most usual answer is something like, "We're still here. Dinosaurs are long gone. So we are more fit!"

That's an irrational answer. You can't judge fitness by whether something is still around. By that logic, anyone who is alive now, no matter how feeble, is more fit than anyone in the past. ("Are you a better baseball player than Babe Ruth? Are you smarter than Marie Curie? Are you wiser than Socrates?" "Sure, they're dead.")

A good way to judge the fitness of dinosaurs versus humans is to see how long species of dinosaurs lasted in the world versus how long *homo sapiens* will have to last to equal that time. Which is likely to be more fit by this way of measuring?

2.18 This kind of statement is a favorite of skeptics, in this case being applied to physics. There are many reputable versions of skepticism. Often, though, people think the sun's rising is doubtful because they reason that just because this event has always occurred in the past doesn't mean it will necessarily occur again tomorrow.

But there is a *logic* to the sun rising: the sun doesn't just happen to rise. The earth is spinning, and for the sun not to "rise" tomorrow, something horrendous would have to happen to the earth to stop it from spinning. It is hard to imagine what could possibly make the earth stop spinning without destroying it, and certainly it couldn't happen without our being well aware of it ahead of time. So if the sun wasn't going to rise tomorrow, we would know it today.

Chapter 3

3.4e An example might be sports that I engage in for fun (my purpose). I might become so fixated on *winning* that it interferes with the fun.

3.5b The question at issue: How can I learn to think through questions and problems in terms of the 8+ elements of reasoning?

3.5d Here are three that sound reasonable:

- What are the major ways *space* is depicted in art?
- What do they have in common and how are they different?
- How do three different modern schools of painting depict *space* in their art?

I might note that *space*, at least on the basis of this chapter, is an f&p concept for understanding art.

3.6d Assumptions:

- That "needs" and "demand" are very different from one another.
- All-or-nothing thinking is not very beneficial.
- The concept *demand* does not encourage all-or-nothing thinking.

3.7c Logically, the person will automatically have more evidence for the second in each pair. Can you see why?

3.7d Here are three:

- Because of this variation, wind and rainfall will also be different from place to place.
- There is a cause (or set of causes) for the variation. → Further question: What are those causes?)
- As a result, living conditions will be very different in different places → crops, clothing, maybe disease.

Your answers may be different. Here are two points to use in evaluating your answers: Are they implications? Are they *important* implications?

3.8e This is different from making a decision that turns out badly because of information you had no reasonable way of knowing.

3.9c Rats, mice, termites, cockroaches, scorpions, rattlesnakes; deer, pheasants, ducks, and geese (in season); calves (veal); and cattle during branding and castration.

3.10d What the drivers *did*—littering or not littering under the various conditions—is information. Why the drivers did not litter is interpretation by the experimenters.

3.11c A test of how fairmindedly you've described Singer's point of view is if Singer would comment on your summary by saying, "Yes, that is exactly what I meant." If you disagree with Singer, a classmate should not be able to tell by reading your summary. (Test it out.)

3.13c For example, if you were born just 200 years ago, you would not have played football, basketball, or baseball; listened to rock music; ridden on a train, car, or bike; lain on a beach for enjoyment; eaten any packaged food. You would never have heard of molecules, bipolar disorder, marketing, bacteria or viruses, genes, galaxies, psychology, plastic, electricity, toilet paper, machine-made clothes, or thousands of other concepts we take entirely for granted.

Chapter 4

4.4 (1) Culture, many argue, is the adhesive binding together of the world's diverse social fabric. (2) A cursory read of the daily newspaper, however, raises questions as to whether the world is literally coming unglued since the frequency and the intensity of (3) cultural conflict seems pervasive and ever-increasing. (4) With the recent rise of global communication systems (satellite TV, movies, video, etc.) stereotypic Western culture is spreading at a rapid pace. While (5) this is willingly accepted by many throughout the world, (6) other groups and countries resist this (7) new form of cultural imperialism through protests, censorship, and restrictions on film, TV, and music.

Elements:

(1) The first sentence is an assumption.

(2) The second sentence identifies a question at issue.

(3) *Cultural conflict* is an important concept in the paragraph.

(4) This sentence is presenting information.

(5) & (6) Both halves of this sentence are presenting information.

(7) The phrase "new form of cultural imperialism" is interpretation; it is based on the concept of political imperialism.

Standards:

Clearness: It's not too clear exactly what the authors mean by "culture." Maybe they will clear that up later. They give some examples of Western culture spreading, and I know there are others. There are a KFC outlet in sight of the pyramids and Coca Cola signs in Red Square.

Accuracy: As far as I can tell, everything is accurate—except for calling it cultural imperialism. To me, the concept of imperialism implies a takeover by force, against the will of the inhabitants. The protests and the rest could not be by too large a percentage of the population. If nobody watched the movies, there would be no cultural imperialism. Moreover, *is* conflict increasing? Or does it just seem that way because it is all over the news?

Importance, relevance: The points made are certainly important because we value diversity among cultures. I don't see how the authors' point about cultural conflict is relevant to the spread of Western culture; they seem like opposites to me.

Sufficiency: The account so far is certainly not sufficient to convince me that the world is literally becoming "unglued." I will wait for the authors to give a more sufficient account as they proceed.

Breadth: I wonder just how broad the dissemination of Western culture is? Does it extend even into poor countries?

Depth: How deep does it go? Is it just *entertainment,* as in the examples? Or does it extend to language, social customs, economic systems? I wonder what underlies this? Why aren't Americans avidly picking up foreign TV and movies?

Precision: Not many details are given: How many protests are there? How much censorship and restriction? Who imposed the censorship? What are the specifics of the "cultural imperialism"?

Chapter 5

Response to the box on p. 163: Evolutionary biologists are the most reliable source for facts about evolutionary biology, within their area of expertise. There is a common fallacy that it's always reasonable to choose the middle road between two extremes.

5.2 There are many ways I could address this question. I'd start by classifying it as a *Category 3* question, requiring different systems. Then, the first element that jumps out is *information:* I need information to answer this question. But information about what?

Not about our common ancestors. Not about the common genes and mechanism of development of humans and *Drosophila*. Not about the medical research that has been done on mice or *Drosophila*. All of those would end up being unhelpful. I do need some good examples from these categories, but, despite how it looked at first, this isn't a question primarily about information.

So I need to *clarify* the *question at issue* for myself. It's a question about the relationship between having common genes and mechanisms (system #1) and an ability to do medical research on one species and transfer it to another (system #2). So it's an *assumption* I'm after: an assumption behind such medical research is that there are common mechanisms. So, as I see it, the question is asking me to evaluate that assumption.

5.3 This question is asking me to regurgitate *information* from the chapter: Category 1.

But I can easily infuse critical thinking into it and get a better grade. It is a question about *context*, the "conditions" that led up to these reformers. So, I will answer it by finding and stating the *main assumption* each of these reformers made. (That will considerably narrow my search.) Then I'll relate each of these five men to one or two of "the political and religious conditions." That will be a description of the *context*. Finally, I'll tell what *conclusions* each reformer drew from that context.

5.4 This is a question looking for a *solution*, a *conclusion:* "Who wins?" *Information* will play a key role: dates, people, agreements, and circumstances. I need to find the relevant law (*information:* in the table of contents there is a section on intoxicated persons), and I need to *interpret* it in relation to this case.

5.5 This is just a detail, strictly Category 1. I'm not going to spend time thinking about it. I'll just look it up in the chapter. It's easy to find, even in this huge chapter. I can look up "Ishtar Terra" in the index. It tells me to go to pages 210–211. That's the only reference to Ishtar Terra, so that's more evidence it is not an important term. (I wonder why the text bothered asking me a question about a detail so insignificant?)

5.6 They asked for a reaction, but I'll give them a reasoned judgment. This is a Category 3 question if there ever was one. I need to feel the pull of the different systems in the question. Clearly (1) I need to spell out the pull of a woman's right to her own body. That's a very strong point, and I need to describe it in such a way that I show its force. Next (2) there is the pull of the fetus's life and why it is important to preserve it. I need to describe the force of that too.

There are assumptions at stake here, and important consequences to any course of action. The judgment will hinge on *accuracy* (e.g., Does the fetus have a full right to life? Does a woman have the right to affect someone else who is alive inside of her?). It will also hinge on which aspect is most *important* for deciding this issue.

5.7 I read this as follows, using the elements and standards:

> (1) The (2) family unit is the foundation of society and the main institution for the growth and advancement of mankind. . . . (3) It is the principal duty of the Islamic government to regard (2) women as the unifying factor of the family unit and its position. (4) They are a factor in bringing the family out of the service of propagating consumerism and exploitation and renewing the vital and valuable (5) duty of motherhood in raising educated human beings. . . . (6) As a result motherhood is accepted as a most profound responsibility in the Muslim viewpoint and will, therefore, (7) be accorded the highest value and generosity.

(1) The first sentence is an *assumption* they are making; the second half is doubtful (*accuracy*). (2) "Family unit" and "women" are *central concepts*: this is how they view the role of women. (3) is an *implication* of (1). (4) states the *purpose* of women, as they see it. That fills in the concept. (5) is an *assumption*: that motherhood is a duty. (6) is a *conclusion* being drawn (but it could also be described as a *consequence*). (7) Definitely a *conclusion*.

5.8 I desperately need f&p concepts. I need to get hold of those f&p concepts that will allow me to think through the logic of rocks: the general *ways they form*, their *structure*, and their *composition*. Once I get a good grasp of those three concepts, that will let me think through most of the terms and summary points in those two chapters.

5.9 Clearly Category 3. This is a question that centers around *points of view*, four different ones. In each case, answering it will rely on how I *interpret* each character, based on the *information* in the text. Then it centers on the *concept* of "real man," as understood by each character.

Notes

To the Instructor

1. Richard Paul, *Critical Thinking: What Every Person Needs to Survive in a Rapidly Changing World,* ed. by A. J. A. Binker (Rohnert Park, CA: Center for Critical Thinking and Moral Critique, 1990).

2. *Critical Thinking: Basic Theory and Instructional Structures* © Foundation for Critical Thinking (Rohnert Park, CA: 1998). www.criticalthinking.org; cct@criticalthinking.org.

3. Jennifer Reed, "Abstract: Effect of a Model for Critical Thinking on Student Achievement in Document Analysis and Interpretation, Argumentative Reasoning, Critical Thinking Dispositions, and History Content in a Community College History Course," Doctoral Dissertation, University of South Florida, 1998. *Dissertation Abstracts International,* 59–11A, 4039.

Chapter 1

1. "A Taxonomy of Critical Thinking Skills and Dispositions," in *Teaching Thinking Skills: Theory and Practice,* ed. Joan Boykoff Baron and Robert J. Sternberg (New York: Freeman, 1987), pp. 9–26. I especially like Ennis's definition, not only because it is the classic one (I believe his first formulation of it came in 1964), but because Bob told me, years later, that it was because of my arguments at the Second International Conference on Critical Thinking at Sonoma State (back in 1982) that he added the "or do" to the end of his definition. I hold deeply that critical thinking needs to be infused in our doings (anything from recycling waste to riding my bike) as much as in our believings.

2. Matthew Lipman, *Thinking in Education* (Cambridge: Cambridge University Press, 1995).

3. The answer is that they stay in prison until they die. "Life" means life.

4. Sarah Blaffer Hrdy, *Mother Nature: A History of Mothers, Infants, and Natural Selection* (New York: Pantheon, 1999), p. 165.

5. Michael Scriven, *Reasoning* (Point Reyes, CA: Edgepress, 1976), p. 26.

6. Dennis J. Sporre, *The Creative Impulse: An Introduction to the Arts* (Upper Saddle River, NJ: Prentice Hall, 2000), p. 15.

7. John Mack Faragher et al., *Out of Many: A History of the American People, II* (Upper Saddle River, NJ: Prentice Hall, 1999), p. 610.

8. The actual quotation is more qualified than the popular slogan. Lord Acton said, "Power tends to corrupt, and absolute power corrupts absolutely." The second half of the statement is still too all-or-nothing for me. Does it imply, for example, that if there is a God who is all-powerful, God must be corrupt?

9. Ian Wright, conversation with author.

Chapter 2

1. Richard Feynman, *What Do You Care What Other People Think?* (New York: Norton, 1988), p. 16.

2. Jennifer Reed, conversation with author.

3. *Tampa Tribune*, September 17, 1996.

4. Hrdy, *Mother Nature: A History of Mothers, Infants, and Natural Selection*, p. xi.

5. Quoted in Paul Heyne, *The Economic Way of Thinking* (New York: Macmillan, 1994), p. xix.

6. Actually they do have a logic: the keyboard was originally designed to *slow down* your typing. That's why the keys are in an "illogical" arrangement that makes you use your weakest fingers to strike the most frequent letters.

7. Charles G. Morris with Albert A. Maisto, *Psychology: An Introduction* (Upper Saddle River, NJ: Prentice Hall, 1999), pp. 5–6.

8. This question comes from Anisa Al-Khatab, conversation with author.

9. The answer is "None of the above." You fall at 32 feet/sec^2. That is tremendously fast. The step breaks, and boom! you're on the ground. It's not like the cartoons where the step breaks and the coyote is suspended in the air before he falls.

   You can hear that objects fall at 32 ft/sec^2 a hundred times, and it never registers just how *fast* that is.

10. The standard answer people usually give is one that makes sense and has a good common-sense logic to it: "Collective farming did not work because people simply do not work as hard when they don't own the land they are working. It stands to reason that people will put a lot more effort into farming the land if they are the ones who make a profit by the results of their hard work."

    Notice the force of the logic in the answer. But notice that the logic loses most of its force if a high percentage of land in the U. S. is owned by large corporations rather than by the people who work the land.

11. Adapted from Kurt Reusser, "Problem Solving Beyond the Logic of Things," cited in A. H. Schoenfeld, "On Mathematics and Sense Making: An Informal Attack on the Unfortunate Divorce of Formal and Informal Mathematics," in J. Voss, D. Perkins, and J. Segal (eds.), *Informal Reasoning and Education* (Hillsdale, NJ: Erlbaum, 1990), pp. 311–343.

12. This is adapted from John J. Macionis, *Sociology* (Upper Saddle River, NJ: Prentice Hall, 1999), pp. 457–459.

13. Gary Armstrong and Philip Kotler, *Marketing: An Introduction* (Upper Saddle River, NJ: Prentice Hall, 2000), pp. 6–7.

14. Lynn Quitman Troyka and Jerold Nudelman, *Steps in Composition* (Upper Saddle River, NJ: Prentice Hall, 1999), p. 31.

15. Ronald J. Ebert and Ricky W. Griffin, *Business Essentials* (Upper Saddle River, NJ: Prentice Hall, 1998), p. iii.

16. Stephen P. Robbins, *Managing Today* (Upper Saddle River, NJ: Prentice Hall, 2000), p. xiii.

Chapter 3

1. Adapted from Richard Paul © The Foundation for Critical Thinking, www.criticalthinking.org; cct@criticalthinking.org. Reprinted with permission.

2. James Monroe and Reed Wicander, *Physical Geology: Exploring the Earth* (Minneapolis: West, 1995), p. 588.

3. *Courage to Change* (New York: Al-Anon, 1992), p. 115.

4. John Adkins Richardson, *Art: The Way It Is* (Englewood Cliffs, NJ: Prentice Hall, 1973), p. 6.

5. Heyne, *The Economic Way of Thinking*, p. 22.

6. Jesse H. Wheeler and J. Trenton Kostbade, *Essentials of World Regional Geography* (Fort Worth, TX: Saunders, 1995), p. 18.

7. Elliot Aronson, *The Social Animal* (New York: Freeman, 1995), p. 30.

8. Thomas A. Mappes and Jane S. Zembaty, *Social Ethics* (New York: McGraw-Hill, 1997), p. 436.

Chapter 4

1. Gerald Nosich, *Reasons and Arguments* (Belmont, CA: Wadsworth, 1982), p. 53.

2. G. Gerbner, M. Morgan, N. Signorelli, "Television Violence Profile no. 16: The Turning Point from Research to Action" (1993), cited in David G. Myers, *Psychology* (New York: Worth, 1995), p. 631.

3. Richard Paul, "Critical Thinking and the Critical Person," in *Thinking: The Second International Conference* (Hillsdale, NJ: Erlbaum, 1987);

reprinted in Paul, *Critical Thinking: What Every Person Needs to Survive*, pp. 107–130.

4. Adapted and expanded from *Critical Thinking: Basic Theory and Educational Structures*, pp. 3–32.

5. Les Rowntree et al., *Diversity Amid Globalization* (Upper Saddle River, NJ: Prentice Hall, 2000), p. 19.

Chapter 5

1. Harrison Brown, *The Human Future Revisited* (New York: Norton, 1978), p. 26.

2. Edward F. Bergman and Tom L. McKnight, *Introduction to Geography* (Upper Saddle River, NJ: Prentice Hall, 1993), p. 148.

3. Troyka and Nudelman, *Steps in Composition*, p. 161.

4. Faragher, *Out of Many*, p. 444.

5. Most factual answers were themselves once the product of reasoned judgment. Facts had to be *discovered*, and discovery is a complex process involving not just one reasoned judgment, but many. Not only that, but facts are of course subject to revision in the light of new information and new explanatory theories. What is factual is often not written in stone.

6. *Critical Thinking: Basic Theory and Instructional Structures*, pp. 4–7.

7. William E. Segall and Anna V. Wilson, *Introduction to Education: Teaching in a Diverse Society* (Upper Saddle River, NJ: Prentice Hall, 1998), p. 170.

8. Kim Flachmann and Michael Flachmann, *The Prose Reader: Essays for Thinking, Reading, and Writing* (Upper Saddle River, NJ: Prentice Hall, 1999), p. 170.

9. Macionis, *Sociology*, p. 143.

10. *Critical Thinking: Basic Theory and Instructional Structures*, p. 3–32.

11. David Krogh, *Biology* (Upper Saddle River, NJ: Prentice Hall, 2000), p. 325.

12. Sporre, *The Creative Impulse*, p. 383.

13. Henry R. Cheeseman, *Contemporary Business Law* (Upper Saddle River, NJ: Prentice Hall, 2000), p. 242.

14. Eric Chaisson and Steve McMillan, *Astronomy Today* (Upper Saddle River, NJ: Prentice Hall, 1999), p. 220.

15. Quoted in Margaret L. King, *Western Civilization: A Social and Cultural History*, *II* (Upper Saddle River, NJ: Prentice Hall, 2000), p. 928.

16. Pamela J. Annas and Robert C. Rosen, *Literature and Society* (Upper Saddle River, NJ: Prentice Hall, 2000), p. 279.

Index

Note: "Ex" before a number refers to exercises with responses.